TRUMPET TECHNIQUE

Trumpet Technique

BY
DELBERT A. DALE

LONDON
OXFORD UNIVERSITY PRESS

OXFORD   NEW YORK

Oxford University Press, Walton Street, Oxford OX2 6DP

OXFORD LONDON GLASGOW NEW YORK
TORONTO MELBOURNE WELLINGTON CAPE TOWN
IBADAN NAIROBI DAR ES SALAAM LUSAKA
KUALA LUMPUR SINGAPORE JAKARTA HONG KONG TOKYO
DELHI BOMBAY CALCUTTA MADRAS KARACHI
ISBN 0 19 318702 7

First published	*1965*
Fifth impression	*1977*
Sixth impression	*1982*

PRINTED IN GREAT BRITAIN
BY J. W. ARROWSMITH LTD., BRISTOL

CONTENTS

NOTE

I am indebted to Mr. William Overton, principal trumpeter of the B.B.C. Symphony Orchestra and Professor of Trumpet at the Royal Academy in London, who read my typescripts and provided valuable criticism and advice. Because of his help in this manner and his additions to the chapter 'The Trumpet in the Symphony Orchestra' I am certain that this book will prove more valuable to a larger number of readers.

FOREWORD

There are at present several fine trumpet etude and method books of all grade levels on the market which are easily available to the trumpet student. Such books will provide sustenance to the student throughout his entire training period, from the very beginning to the advanced stage. The college student, moreover, may refer to hundreds of theses (through inter-library loan) devoted to particular aspects of the trumpet; including works on the history and construction of the instrument, its use in ensembles and in the band and orchestra, others on various technical aspects of playing, and some on certain aspects of the repertoire, etc.

It is, though, somewhat difficult to find a simple handbook of trumpet playing which will touch, however lightly, on most or all of these factors. It has been my purpose here to provide such a book, though emphasis has been placed on those technical aspects which are of immediate and practical use to the average student. It was my aim to present a short (and economical) textbook of some of the technical problems one may meet in the study of the trumpet and to suggest some solutions to those problems. The chapters on embouchure, breathing, tone, etc., should be of particular benefit to beginning and intermediate students. And with the addition of such chapters as those on the use of the trumpet in the orchestra and on repertoire, I have tried to make it useful to even the most advanced students of the trumpet. It is my sincere hope that all students of the trumpet might find in this book something of personal value to them. If only a few do, then my desires will have been gratified.

I have purposely left out the subject of transposition, though it is indeed a very important aspect of the trumpet player's technique. Transposition is mainly a problem for the orchestral player; others are only seldom confronted with having to transpose their parts from their instrument's original 'reading' key. Though some teachers like to start transposition study fairly early in their student's training, it is of little practical value except for purposes of simple ear training. The jazz trumpeter sometimes finds it necessary to play something in a new and strange key to him, but this too is a case of being able to 'hear' in any key (relative pitch), which has little to do with the actual mechanics of transposition. In the chapter entitled 'The Trumpet in the Orchestra', it is my thesis that the orchestral trumpeter is concerned with not one, but several differently pitched trumpets. Thus to present a detailed explanation of all the transpositions and the several different thought-processes involved, would require many, many explanatory examples, too many for the limits of this short book. Besides, I contend that transposition is really not technically difficult for most students, though it may seem so at the outset of its study. It only requires many hours of 'reading experience'. It is not that the student must learn to read in a foreign language; it is more like having to read just one language IN CAPITAL LETTERS or in small letters (or *in italicized ones*).

It is clear that any treatise on technique is bound to attract a certain amount of criticism from those who find their personal theories in direct discord to those presented. Certainly I don't mean to present this book as a 'compleat' encyclopedia of trumpet playing. None the less, I feel that most theories presented here are of basic use to most students of the trumpet. And if the student finds that the principles advocated herein are somewhat contradictory to his own (or to his teacher's), I can only suggest that he make his own comparisons and experiments. I encourage all students to search continually for as many solutions to their problems as possible, for only through a great amount of investigation and analysis can each player finally settle on the perfect solution for himself.

THE INSTRUMENT AND
MOUTHPIECE

A cursory glance into the history of the modern trumpet should, I feel, be beneficial to the aspiring trumpet student. By looking back, he may grasp a new insight into the structural problems of the instrument, how those particular problems affect and influence the player's 'technique', and lastly how he may adjust to, and overcome, such defects as are inherent to the trumpet.

For all practical purposes, we may begin at that point in the history of the trumpet when it finally became a 'musical' instrument (in contradistinction to those variously named 'trumpets' used prior to this time mainly as mere signalling devices by armies and at various ceremonial rites), and when the possibilities were being explored of using the trumpet in concert performance. This took place some time during the Renaissance; that is, within the two-hundred-year period between A.D. 1400–1600. Prior to that time the prototypes of the trumpet were very simple instruments capable of only one or two pitches. Obviously, for a musical performance, something better was needed.

It was gradually discovered that by lengthening the instrument and using a proper mouthpiece, the higher partials of the overtone series natural to all cup-mouthpiece instruments could be produced. Thus, by the time of the Baroque era (seventeenth and eighteenth centuries), the trumpet had evolved into an instrument some seven or eight feet in length, wound around on itself. By playing within the range from the 3rd partial up to about the 15th partial (a few very outstanding players could evidently reach even higher notes), it could be used very effectively (see Ex. 1). Indeed, as the trumpet is still usually defined as an instrument possessing a bore which is mainly cylindrical in shape, the Baroque trumpet was, and remains, the most aristocratic member of the whole family of trumpets: approximately

four-fifths of the length of this trumpet was completely
cylindrical. As we shall see in the following chapter, the
splendid brilliance and radiant tone of these long trumpets
cannot, unfortunately, be duplicated on our modern-day
shorter trumpets.

Ex. 1

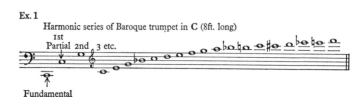

Harmonic series of Baroque trumpet in C (8ft. long)

Fundamental

Of course, the Baroque trumpet also had its serious draw-
backs; several of the partials were quite out-of-tune, and
since it was a valveless instrument and effective only in the
upper partials, the task of the trumpet player was certainly
a difficult one. This, plus the fact that composers were
constantly seeking new uses for the trumpet which
demanded a greater flexibility, led to refinements in
construction. They were (1) the invention of a slide-
trumpet (German, 'zugtrompete'), which had a substantial
vogue in Germany and later in England, (2) a trumpet that
could change keys by inserting different sized crooks; and,
later (3) the invention of the valve trumpet. Those in the
first two categories had obvious faults due to their un-
wieldiness and their popularity was fairly short-lived.
Around the beginning of the nineteenth century, however,
several almost simultaneous inventions pertaining to the
valve led to an instrument quite similar to that which we
use today. Within the next hundred years several trumpets,
pitched in various keys, had short periods of popularity, but
gradually the B♭ trumpet (approximately $4\frac{1}{2}$ ft. in length)
became the most generally used. And though in recent
years the C trumpet (slightly smaller yet than the B♭) has
somewhat replaced the B♭ in the larger U.S. and French
symphony orchestras, the B♭ remains the preferred instrument in most of the British and European orchestras. In

brass bands and in jazz bands and studio orchestras, too, the B♭ is exclusively used.

To interested students seeking additional information on the history of the trumpet, I recommend them to look into the history of the 'cornett' (a wooden instrument with keys and tone holes much like our present day woodwind instruments, but played with a cup-mouthpiece), the 'keyed bugle' of Anton Weidinger (for whom Haydn wrote his immortal concerto) and the whole family of bugles which evolved into the modern flügelhorn and cornet.

Some facts regarding the construction and tonal qualities of the trumpet and cornet

The prevalence (or absence) of upper partials in a given tone distinguishes one tone colour from another. That is why we discern a difference between the sound of a piccolo, for instance, and that of a tuba. The chief characteristic of most brass (cup-mouthpiece) instruments is that there is an enormous wealth of these upper partials. The construction of the instrument has of course a large bearing on this tone factor, and by making slight changes in the design of the instrument, it is possible not only to change the tonal timbre, but also to vary the response of these upper harmonics in playing them as notes. Thus, an instrument with a 'large' bore, somewhat conical in shape and played with a deep cup mouthpiece, will possess a warmer and darker tone than one which has a narrow and mainly cylindrical bore and played with a shallow mouthpiece. This is the outstanding difference (besides the addition of valves) between the modern short trumpet and its ancestor, the long trumpet. Herein lies also the difference between the trumpet and the cornet, for the latter has an even more conical bore than the trumpet, and is usually played with a deeper cup mouthpiece.

Both the modern trumpet and the cornet, however, have similar defects due to the similarity of design and because they share a common fundamental (B♭). It is impossible to build a three-valve instrument so that all of the approximately thirty notes in the normal playing range will be perfectly in tune with each other. For instance, the fourth partial (see Ex. 2) on each valve combination (open, 2, 1, 12, 23, 13, 123) is quite naturally flat. Although this can be corrected to some extent in manufacturing the instrument, when it is, other tones are adversely affected. Most present-day trumpets thus fall into two basic classes of 'pitch-patterns' (see Ex. 3).

Ex. 2

Modern B♭ trumpet harmonic series (written C sounds concert B♭)

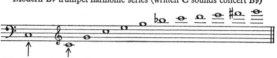

Fundamental 1st Partial etc.

Ex. 3

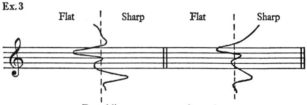

Dotted line represents true intonation

Moreover, though the separate valve slides are fairly well in tune when played singly, when they are used in combination they become gradually sharper as more and more tubing is used. Thus, the valve combination 123 is sharper at every point on the scale than when any of the three are played by themselves. For this reason, most piston valve trumpets come equipped with a third valve slide finger ring and a thumb key or ring on the first valve slide in order to help correct these deficiencies. Added to this is the fact that with only one bell and one mouthpipe to serve seven differently pitched valve combinations (in effect, seven different sized trumpets), the tone varies as more and more tubing is used. This is because of the different relationship between the bore and the total amount of tubing, or length, of the instrument. Thus the tone of the open trumpet will be more sonorous and responsive than a tone produced through the use of valves.

Selection of a good trumpet or cornet

All of the above must be taken into consideration in purchasing an instrument. First in importance, I believe, is the matter of intonation. The student must choose an instrument that is as much in tune as possible, when *he* plays upon it. All brass instruments are similar to double-reed instruments in that the player's two lips act as the reed. Obviously everyone has a distinct style of producing a tone on the trumpet. One will play with a tense and somewhat pinched embouchure. He will normally have to pull his main tuning slide out farther than the player who uses a looser lip setting. As we have learned in the preceding section, adding tubing to the natural length of the instrument (or pulling out slides) seriously affects the intonation and response of the instrument. Therefore, the intonation of the instrument must be checked against the player's normal playing pitch. If the instrument's main tuning slide must be pulled out quite far to agree with this pitch, then it should not be chosen. Moreover, some slide must be left (to push in), in order to raise the pitch when the occasion demands. In a later chapter, more will be said concerning the adjustment of intonation.

Next in importance is the general response of the instrument. Does it seem fairly easy to get a note to speak without having to 'blast'? Does the resultant tone have a vibrancy to it, neither too shrill and brilliant nor too dull and colourless? With respect to this, it should be remembered that the mouthpiece has a great influence on these factors of tone, intonation, and response of the instrument. Often the student will blame the instrument for defects which are in fact caused by a poor mouthpiece.

It should also be noted that the demands placed on a trumpet by a professional player are not those required or even desired by an amateur or beginning student. Most players, even advanced ones, and certainly all those of lesser abilities, must not purchase a 'large' bore (in England and Europe—'very large' bore) trumpet, for this would be just as bad as buying the proverbial 'pea-shooter' or small-bore trumpet. Even many physically mature players cannot cope with an over-large horn. Thus, a 'medium' bore, or at most, a 'medium-large' bore, should be selected for the beginner.

In purchasing a used instrument, be sure that the valves are in good condition. If they can be wiggled sideways in the valve casing then they are too loose and will leak, and considerable efficiency of the instrument will be lost. Be sure that the metal has not worn thin through too much use, or by several overhaul and relacquer jobs.

Many teachers recommend that all beginning students start on the cornet. Because of its slightly different bore relationship and design, it has more resistance built into the instrument which makes it somewhat easier to blow and gives it a little more flexibility than the trumpet. Besides, the beginning student will have more of an opportunity to participate in band playing to which this instrument is better suited. This author would advise any young student to start on the cornet, if for no other reason than that it is simpler to hold and that this will in turn aid the young player in developing a good posture while playing.

Finally, the student should seek the best professional advice available (from either his teacher or some competent local player) in choosing a proper instrument.

Care of the instrument

It would certainly be ridiculous to purchase an expensive instrument unless one intends to take good care of it. Besides, if properly taken care of, and cleaned regularly, it need only take a few minutes of one's time. Weekly the instrument should be flushed out with luke-warm water. Some say that soapy water should be used, but I feel that this is unnecessary if plain water is used *regularly*. First fill the instrument with water, depressing the valves, and then blow it out. Do this several times. Then, taking out all the valve slides, simply hold them under a faucet for a few minutes each. There are small brushes available which may be run through the main tuning slide and through the mouthpiece. After doing this, the valves must be taken out, wiped with a soft cloth (also carefully run a soft cloth through the valve casings), and re-oiled. The slides must be wiped and greased again with a very thin coating of Vaseline or slide grease. Be sure not to let any excess get into the open tubing. The valves should be oiled daily with a special valve oil obtainable from any dealer. Caution: Never use ordinary lubricating oil. And be certain that the third valve slide and first valve slide move effortlessly since these will be often used on the out-of-tune notes. If this cleaning procedure is done weekly, then no other effort need be made.

The mouthpiece

I shall address my remarks in this chapter specifically to the orchestral trumpeter, or to the student who intends to pursue this type of work. The jazz player or 'high-note artist' in one of the modern jazz bands very often depends upon a somewhat 'unorthodox' mouthpiece to be able to meet his special requirements. Especially in the larger bands, he is chiefly concerned with finding a mouthpiece with which he may last through a long and tiring job and one which will make his upper range easier. Unfortunately, this is often done somewhat at the expense of good tone quality. Of course if such a player were to use a 'large' mouthpiece, i.e. one with an extremely wide or deep cup and with a large throat or bore, he would find it practically impossible to endure the long hours of his work. He must of necessity choose a smaller-type mouthpiece.

The symphonic trumpeter is mainly concerned with a mouthpiece that will afford him a large volume of tone, more flexibility, and which will allow him to play both fortissimo and pianissimo in all registers over a shorter duration of playing time. He is also very concerned with sureness of attack and response.

Before going on to the selection of a proper mouthpiece, we must first examine the various parts of a mouthpiece and find out how each influences the overall capabilities of an average mouthpiece. It must be noted that all of these various parts of the mouthpiece are inter-related, and one separate part is important only in its relation to the rest of the mouthpiece (see Fig. 1).

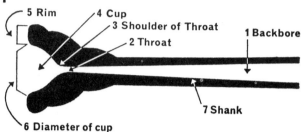

Throat and backbore

This lower section of the mouthpiece has much to do with both the intonation of the mouthpiece and to its resistance. If the resistance is increased or decreased, naturally there will be also a marked difference in the flexibility and endurance of the player. The backbore, or that part of the mouthpiece which extends from the throat to the lower end of the shank, can flare out rapidly or it can be of a more straight or cylindrical nature. Usually only this factor of the mouthpiece is different between the cornet and trumpet mouthpiece; the cup and rim generally the same for mouthpieces of both instruments. If the backbore expands rapidly (that is, a larger bore), the tone will naturally be larger in volume. This, however, will decrease the resistance of the mouthpiece, having the effect of 'pulling' the player's lips into the mouthpiece, and his endurance will suffer comparatively. The tone will also be more difficult to control, especially in playing pianissimo. A small backbore will have the opposite tendencies. The resistance will be increased, thereby allowing the player more endurance, but the tone will be smaller, though more easily controlled. Any extreme in the length or shape of the backbore will also influence the intonation of the instrument. For instance, a too small backbore will cause the high register to be flat, and here too, the opposite extreme will have its corresponding faults.

The backbore should ideally fit the bore of the mouthpipe of the instrument. This is my argument against using

European-made mouthpieces on American-made instruments and vice versa, since both Europe and America have more or less basic standardized sizes for their instruments and mouthpieces. The end of the mouthpiece shank should meet fairly well with the end of the mouthpipe of the instrument. When the difference here is too great (or if the mouthpiece doesn't fit solidly and firmly into the instrument), and if the player has a mouthpiece he is attached to, it is possible in some cases to have a whole new lead-pipe put on the trumpet to correct this situation. Many manufacturers are equipped to do this. I myself have twice ordered instruments from two European manufacturers, detailing the size of the mouthpiece I intended to use with their instrument, and in both cases I was satisfied with the results.

The throat of the mouthpiece is generally cylindrical in shape. The length of the straight portion of the throat will decide the intonation of the mouthpiece and instrument generally. It is necessary to keep the throat and backbore very clean by occasionally running a small brush through it, since even the smallest particle of dirt will affect the intonation and response of the mouthpiece. Many careless students do not take care of their mouthpiece and one often sees a mouthpiece whose shank is dented, with of course the same harmful effects.

The player who has occasion to change instruments will find it necessary in most cases to switch mouthpieces also, since the bore relationship of the mouthpiece to the instrument is so important. It is very difficult to find a mouthpiece that will play equally well on two different-sized instruments. A really good C trumpet mouthpiece, for example, will probably throw a B♭ instrument quite sharp, and vice versa. Piccolo trumpets in F, G, and B♭ especially need to be played with a smaller type mouthpiece because of their extremely small bore. Thus, a professional trumpeter quite often will play on a screw-rim mouthpiece, whereby, having the rim that is most comfortable to him, he can immediately change to different sized cups and backbores as the instrument demands.

Assuming that the instrument is a good professional model instrument, bad intonation can often be caused by the mouthpiece not being proportioned correctly to the instrument. In some cases this can be remedied by lengthening or shortening the throat or backbore a little. Only a thoroughly competent mouthpiece maker would be equipped to do this, of course.

Cup diameter

The diameter of the cup (taken from the inside of the rim, where the rim meets the bowl-shaped part) decides just how much of the lips will vibrate, thereby directly affecting the tone and flexibility. A large cup diameter will allow a larger portion of the lips to vibrate inside the mouthpiece and will thus result in a larger volume of tone. Vincent Bach, one of the world's leading mouthpiece manufacturers, recommends the use of 'as large a cup diameter as the player can endure to play upon', and this is indeed very sound advice. A large cup diameter has a tendency to open the lips of the player a little more, assuring a clearer tone quality. However, the player whose lips are not yet muscularly developed and whose lips tend thus to enter the mouthpiece when playing, should be particularly careful not to use a mouthpiece whose diameter and cup volume is so large as to encourage such a habit. Nevertheless, a large cup diameter will permit more freedom of lip movement in the mouthpiece and therefore it should to some extent feel more comfortable on the lips than a mouthpiece so small as to actually cramp their movements.

At first, the player switching to a larger cup diameter mouthpiece will find the higher notes a little more difficult to produce, but with a reasonable amount of effort in lip training, he will discover that he can soon regain control of the higher register. Whereas a smaller mouthpiece to some extent encourages the use of mouthpiece pressure against the lip, the student will find that this added pressure for high notes will be of no help with a large mouthpiece. However, he will soon learn to negotiate the higher notes correctly through proper lip movement.

Cup volume and shape—shoulder of throat

If one could cut a hundred trumpet mouthpieces in

half or could take clay impressions of their cups, he would probably be very surprised: for although there are limits to the overall volume capacity of the cup, the variety of shapes which can produce a standard volume is almost endless. There are V-shaped cups, bowl-shaped cups, ones with a sharp or rounded shoulder, double-cups, etc. I have made myself a set of three cup-measuring devices out of German one pfennig coins with which I can get a pretty fair idea of the largeness or smallness of most trumpet mouthpieces.

Generally speaking, the larger the volume of the cup, the more full and dark the tone. This is particularly true if the shoulder of the throat is open. Thus, a V-shaped cup will have a mellower tone quality, and though some cornet soloists prefer this deeper cup, it is not very satisfactory when used on the trumpet. Most symphonic trumpeters, and especially studio musicians, will use a more bowl-shaped cup in order to get the brilliant sound necessary for their work.

A shallower cup will brighten the tone and response and attacks will be easier, and if the point where the shoulder meets the throat is sharp and not too rounded or flaring, the attacks will be easier. Fig. 2A has a quite sharp curve going into the throat, whereas Fig. 2B has practically no shoulder at all.

Fig 2

Bite

The 'bite' or inner edge of the rim, or the point where the rim meets the cup, also is important because of its influence on the precision of attack. A sharp edge here will aid greatly the precision of attacks and response of the tone. A mouth-piece that does not have a sufficiently sharp edge at this point will not allow the lips to vibrate freely; and this should be particularly kept in mind in selecting a mouth-piece to perform extremely high parts, i.e. F, G, and B♭ piccolo trumpet parts. Preferably the 'bite' should be set low into the cup so as not to cut the lips when applying slight pressure from the mouthpiece.

Rim curvature and diameter

This is the part of the mouthpiece which comes in direct contact with the lips, so comfort is the all-important factor to consider here. Nevertheless certain factors must be kept in mind, since even though a mouthpiece might feel very comfortable on the lips at first touch, it may prove, after only several minutes of playing, to be disastrous to the lip. For example, though a wide cusion-rim mouthpiece may at first seem particularly comfortable, it is a fact that such a rim will tend to clamp down the lip muscles, depriving the player of flexibility. And since the mouthpiece rim is large and spread over a larger area of the lip, the excess pressure is not too noticeable at first. The player will thus tend naturally to use this added pressure to make up for his lost flexibility. Only too late does he realize that he has indeed used too much pressure; his lips are swollen and he must quit playing. The use of a narrower rim mouthpiece will remind the student immediately if too much pressure is being used. The use of a narrow rim mouthpiece then will give the player more flexibility such as is demanded in playing intervals, arpeggios, etc., but an extremely narrow rim will cut the lips, especially if the player's lips are not very muscular. In other words, for most players, a medium wide rim is the best compromise between the cutting effect of the narrow rim and the bad habits that accrue from using a too-wide rim.

Specially made or custom-built mouthpieces

There are now hundreds of different-sized mouthpieces on the market, readily available to the student. For this reason, specially-made mouthpieces need not normally be considered. To begin with, the extra cost of such a mouthpiece does not ensure that it will be any better than a regular stock model, and if the mouthpiece is damaged or lost, it might not be readily replaceable. Contoured mouthpieces, the rims of which are curved to fit the overbite of the top teeth, are also absolutely unnecessary, unless the student's dento-facial structure is so extreme as to hinder normal adjustment to a standard model mouthpiece. However, such a student probably shouldn't be playing the trumpet anyway.

Selection of the mouthpiece

It is very difficult for a player to select the mouthpiece which is best suited to his embouchure and style of playing. Even taking into consideration what has been said in the last section, it is hard to make even very general statements regarding proper mouthpiece selection.

The beginning student is basically interested in obtaining results as quickly as possible, even though his embouchure is not yet fully developed and his lip muscles are weak. But just because these lip muscles are so deplorably weak and delicate, it is extremely important to find at the very beginning a mouthpiece that is as suitable as possible. Preference should definitely be given to a good medium-sized mouthpiece—one that will be small enough to aid rapid development of the difficult high register in the early weeks, but large enough to allow the student's lips to develop normally and to produce a good tone. The inexperienced player will often select a mouthpiece solely because the high notes are easier, but that alone is not enough to warrant selecting a particular mouthpiece.

Of course it is foolish to shop for a mouthpiece that will do all the work. The mastery of the trumpet, it hardly need be said, depends mostly on the talent and industriousness of the student and mere physical properties can only aid or hinder his progress. It would be equally foolish to select a certain mouthpiece just because some friend or famous trumpeter used it and seems to get good results. Certainly the selection of a mouthpiece must be a personal choice. If the beginning student has adequate advice to begin with and selects a proper-sized mouthpiece, he will have little reason to change mouthpieces for several years, or until the time his embouchure is fully developed and he can physically cope with a larger and more professional model mouthpiece. Changing mouthpieces constantly is a very bad habit. By using one mouthpiece over a long period of time, the student can train the same set of muscles consistently and constantly: witness the accuracy of the professional trumpeter, who in all probability, has used the same mouthpiece for ten or twenty years or more.

The advanced student who has already developed his lip muscles correctly and is soon preparing to enter the professional field will desire a larger mouthpiece. Through diligent study he will soon be able to strengthen his embouchure the necessary amount and can achieve the larger tone and greater flexibility demanded of the professional player.

Finally, the main consideration should be tone quality. Ease of playing should be of secondary importance to this. It must be kept in mind, that though many have tried, no one has yet found the 'perfect' mouthpiece; at best a good mouthpiece can only be a compromise of the basic aspects of the mouthpiece, the student's age and achievement level, and his physical characteristics.

We may conclude that a correctly chosen mouthpiece can definitely benefit the student's progress, just as a poorly chosen one will hinder it. I believe all students should seek the advice of a truly competent teacher or professional player before buying a mouthpiece: nevertheless the final selection must absolutely be a personal choice.

II

EMBOUCHURE

It need hardly be mentioned that, to wind-players of all sorts, embouchure is of absolutely primary importance. The woodwind player has several keys on his instrument which can aid progression from one register to another, or even from one tone quality (or intonation) to another. But the trumpeter (with only three pitch-changing mechanisms to help him) must rely upon his embouchure not only to negotiate notes in the different registers, but also to give him basic control over tone, flexibility, intonation, etc. Thus the trumpet player's embouchure in some measure takes on duties that the woodwind player may give to the note-holes and keys and to the reed of his instrument. For, as I have stated previously, the trumpeter's two lips do indeed represent exactly (in the matter of producing tonal vibration) the double reed of the woodwind instrument.

Practically all the trumpet student's technical progress will depend directly upon the efficiency of his embouchure. It has been my experience that students with a good embouchure can, through diligent study, surmount all other technical problems. There are, however, a few that seem never to be able to grasp how the embouchure must be formed to operate effectively. And most of these are students who never got started correctly (that is, lacked the advice of a competent teacher) and who have developed so many bad embouchure habits, that breaking them is virtually an impossibility. Therefore, a student of trumpet, no matter what his age or degree of ability, must forever be concerned with the correct function of his embouchure if he expects any measure of success. It is here that we must begin our study of 'trumpet technique'.

Dento-facial factors

Most people have dento-facial irregularities of some sort: over- or under-sized lower jaw, teeth which are crowded, protruding, or spaced far apart, teeth which are extremely large or small, lips which are extremely small, thick, or thin, and lip textures which are unusually weak and flabby. Of course, some fortunate students have fairly normal relationships of jaw, teeth, and lip. They should normally experience few difficulties regarding their trumpet embouchure. But large irregularities of any sort will most probably interfere with correct embouchure adjustment. So I suggest that the student analyse his own physical structure to begin with, for it is quite possible that a problem in embouchure adjustment may be caused by some little deficiency here. Those who do find some such irregularities in their physical make-up should not be disappointed, however, since most such minor deficiencies can be easily remedied, providing only the student is aware of them.

Ideally the trumpet student should have at least four strong and even front teeth, and as these are the base of the mouthpiece, the more square and flat they are the better. Students with crowded and overlapping front teeth often experience irritation of the lips when slight mouthpiece pressure is used. Mild spacing of the teeth evidently does not require any special embouchure adjustment, but of course extreme spacing of the front teeth would be undesirable.

Discrepancies in the form or size of the jaw will affect the positioning of the teeth and lips, which in turn serve as the support of the mouthpiece. Students with severe retrusion or protrusion of the lower jaw can expect most of their embouchure difficulties to originate from this. There is a much larger percentage of people with retrusion of the lower jaw; and among such trumpet students embouchure problems are very prevalent. However, retrusion or protrusion, if not exaggerated, can usually be corrected by learning to 'position' the jaw. And although this may at first seem unnatural and awkward, the student can in time make it habitual to the point where it seems the natural thing to do.

Ex. A shows a player with a retruded lower jaw, and as the foundation (lips and teeth) of the mouthpiece is slanted, it is natural for this player to play with his instrument pointed downward. Ex. B shows a base which is directly perpendicular, and then naturally the instrument will point directly out. A player such as Ex. A will tend to let his lips enter the mouthpiece, especially in fortissimo playing. The inner edge of the mouthpiece rim is, or should be, fairly sharp, and this sharp edge will then cut the lip and the player's attack and endurance will suffer. A player such as B will allow his lips to lie more on the flat surface of the rim and his lips will not tend so much to enter the mouthpiece. Thus A must try to thrust out his lower jaw so that his teeth are more or less directly in line with each other, if he is to enjoy the advantages of B.

Fig 3

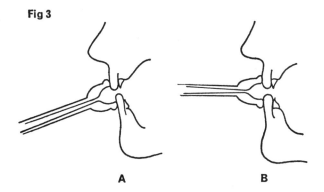

A   B

Finally, let me say that though dento-facial character-istics must certainly be considered in starting the beginner, it is a fact that many students with seemingly extreme physical disadvantages can adapt themselves remarkably well, providing they are aware of their problems and have the talent and industriousness to surmount them.

Placing the mouthpiece

Much attention must be given to the correct placing of the mouthpiece on the lips. It cannot simply be haphazardly set on the lips; rather the student must find the one ideal position that will produce the best results for him. The mouthpiece must not feel merely perched on the lip. There must be a sensation of a 'grip', as though the mouthpiece were sitting in a groove, and so that it feels like a natural extension of the lip muscles rather than a cold piece of inflexible metal pressing on the lips.

As the lips are very flexible and pliable, their appearance outside the mouthpiece and their actual shape inside the mouthpiece may be very different. Thus I suggest that, for practice purposes, the student occasionally uses a cutaway rim, so that he may see how his lips are operating inside the mouthpiece. As to the vertical placing of the mouthpiece, we find that professional players vary slightly in the proportion of lower and upper lip in the mouthpiece. I am of the opinion that the lips should as nearly as possible cross the mouthpiece at the point of widest diameter, and that the farther this lip line (or aperture) is removed from this diameter, the more difficult it will be to produce either the extreme high or the low register, depending upon which way it is shifted and upon the player's style of playing. Certainly the largest volume of tone will be produced by an aperture extending over this largest diameter. This is my personal theory, but I concede that the 'feel' of the correct placing outlined in the preceding paragraph remains of primary importance.

Horizontally the mouthpiece should be placed in the middle, as the tension of the lip muscles will then be equally balanced. Sometimes, though, overlapping or irregular tooth formation makes it necessary to play slightly off-centre. In cases of this sort, the student probably should not change his embouchure unless his teacher strongly recommends a change. If he has good flexibility and control and a good tone, he should probably remain in his most natural position. Many students who start without lessons from a qualified teacher, begin to play off centre, even though their teeth and jaw factors are entirely normal. This is another matter. Probably 90 per cent. of such students can rapidly switch to the centre (also with the help of a competent teacher) and immediately learn to play as well and usually much better than they could before.

After finding the most suitable and comfortable position of the mouthpiece on the lips, the student must take care always to place it in the same position. By doing so he can consistently develop the same set of muscles and will more quickly learn how to control his embouchure.

Function of lips and lip muscles

The important factor here is not so much the size or thickness of the lips (although extremely short or very thick-lipped persons would naturally have more than the normal difficulties), but the texture and muscular flexibility of the lips. Lip flexibility can be somewhat tested by having the beginning student 'buzz' on the mouthpiece, or by having him play simple lip slurs on the instrument.

The upper lip does most of the vibrating, and tension on this lip will govern the speed of the vibration. The shorter and faster the vibrating area moves, the higher will be the resultant pitch. An infinitesimal portion of the lower part of the upper lip must enter the course of the air stream in order to cause it to vibrate. And this portion of the upper lip must be a 'controllable' part of the lip . . . not the fleshy or reddish inner side of the lip.

Fig 4

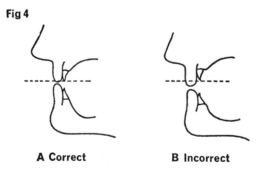

A Correct   **B Incorrect**

Thus, with the upper lip slightly rolled in, the lower edge of this lip should be more or less on the same line as the lower edge of the upper teeth. See Exs. A and B above. If this upper lip hangs too far down past the edge of the upper teeth, having no support there, obviously the impact of the air stream will drive it into the mouthpiece, resulting in tonal distortion and poor endurance.

The labial frenum which connects the upper lip to the gums extends to the inner lower part of the upper lip, and the muscular tissue surrounding this causes most people's upper lip to sag or protrude slightly, right in the centre of the lip. This 'lobe' is a constant source of trouble, because the greater concentration of muscle and fleshy tissue is placed in the exact spot where the embouchure's aperture must be formed.

Fig 5

This 'lobe' must not be allowed to interfere with the air stream, or protrude over the opening between the lips. By slightly rolling in this section of the lip, the upper lip can be held against the teeth in a more or less straight line. Try this experiment. 'Buzz' lips while watching in a mirror, so that you can both see and 'feel' the exact point where the air is striking the upper lip. If that point is on the outer dull-reddish part of the lip then your lip is sufficiently rolled in. If that point is on the inner fleshy part of the lip then it needs to be rolled in slightly more. The tendency for this centre section of the upper lip to slip out is greater in the low register and even more in fortissimo or tongued passages when percussive puffs of air slap against the tip of the lip. For the same reason, the tongue must not be allowed to come in direct contact with the lips in the normal tonguing action.

Allowing for muscular tension and relaxation, then, the upper lip should theoretically remain more or less stationary *vis-à-vis* the teeth. Especially, it should not rise and lower much when the pitch ascends or descends.

The lower lip is responsible for adjusting the size of the aperture, or opening, between the lips. Thus, the lower lip should tighten slightly in ascending, thereby increasing the tension on the upper lip; and it should relax in descending, taking the pressure off of the upper lip and creating a larger aperture. For balanced tension the lower lip should ideally be directly opposite, that is perpendicular to, the upper lip, moving directly up or down as the case may be. But even though the muscles of the lower lip are tightened or drawn up to create tension on the upper lip, it is not necessary to move the chin in the process. Keep the chin down.

As far as I have been able to observe, players have two basically different types of lip texture and lip function. And there seems to be a definite relationship between basic lip texture and embouchure adjustment. First there are players with lips of a tough and fibrous nature (generally thin-lipped persons), whose lips do not tend to enter the mouthpiece but are firm enough to stay close to the teeth withstanding the air pressure. And secondly, players with softer, fleshier lips (usually thick-lipped persons) whose lips do definitely have a tendency to enter the mouthpiece when playing. Furthermore, I have noticed that those in the first category generally have fewer embouchure problems whereas the latter have more, and must therefore be more 'choosy' in selecting a proper mouthpiece.

The centre of the lips: the aperture

The centre of the lips is where most of the attention should focus in any study of the embouchure—attention both physical and mental. In teaching my pupils muscle focusing, I compare the aperture between the lips to the hub of a wheel, with all the facial and lip muscles representing the spokes pointing towards the hub. Any muscle pulling or tension in an opposite direction from the centre will simply lessen the effort than can be utilized beneficially in the centre. Actually, the centre of the lips should be somewhat 'puckered', but the lips should still be held firmly against the teeth and not protrude.

Though the lips do vibrate both by themselves and against each other at the sides of the aperture, they should not touch in the centre itself. And this opening is or should be quite similar to the open end of an oboe reed. In fact, we may say that the aperture used in producing the high register is like that of an oboe reed, whereas the one used for the lower register is like that of a bassoon reed. Thus the shape of the opening is similar in both registers, but enlarged or decreased by muscular relaxation or tension.

In order to keep this basic standard opening on all notes, one must remember not simply to pinch the lips together in order to get the high notes. This results in a thin tone in the upper register and leads to the use of unnecessary pressure.

In moving from one register to another in intervals or scalewise passages, there is also an accompanying change in the direction of the air stream entering the mouthpiece, and of course, some action in the centre of the lips must make this possible. It is generally agreed, I believe, that the higher notes are produced by the air stream hitting close to the inside edge of the rim of the mouthpiece, whereas the lower notes will be produced by blowing straight into the mouthpiece. This can be tested by placing the hand directly in front of the mouth, in the way of the air stream, and then 'buzzing' the lips, gradually tightening the lip muscles and raising the pitch of the buzz and then descending by relaxing the lip tension. The direction of the air stream, it will be found, will indeed change, and the same sort of action of the centre lip muscles should take place when using the mouthpiece and instrument.

I have often suggested in this chapter that the student 'buzz' his lips in experimenting with his embouchure. I believe this to be a wonderful exercise for the study of the embouchure, to 'loosen' up the lips in warm-ups and to develop lip tension. But I must point out that this 'buzz' embouchure is not the same as the normal 'playing' embouchure. Try this experiment. 'Buzz' a middle G (second line) and while continuing the 'buzz', bring the mouthpiece and instrument gradually up to the lips to their normal pressure-position. The pitch will rise and a middle C or E will probably result. Now buzz a middle C and do the same thing. An even higher note will result with the normal light pressure. We may conclude then that the normal playing aperture will be much larger than that of the 'buzz' aperture of the same pitch, due to the tension on the lips caused by simple mouthpiece pressure. And let me say that this playing aperture must always be formed by the lips prior to starting the tone, not by the onrush of air seeking an outlet through the lips.

Through diligent lip training and commonsense study

of correct lip movements, the student will gradually get the 'feel' of the mouthpiece on the lip. He must learn to recognize certain feelings and sensations regarding his embouchure when playing certain passages or lip-training studies. Though the trumpeter cannot of course actually see his lips functioning inside the mouthpiece, he must acquire a mental image or picture of the various lip movements before he can hope to have absolute control of his embouchure. The value of this mental picture, and the simple physical sensations concerning correct lip function cannot, I believe, be over-emphasized. It is indeed very important.

The corners of the mouth

The corners of the mouth should remain in more or less their natural position, held firmly and anchored in a stationary position against the teeth, so that they will not stretch outward or pull in towards the centre. Still, though they are held firm, they must not be overly tense or hard, for any excessive muscle effort here will simply detract from the control needed in the centre of the lips. Experiment with the corners in different positions: failure in endurance can often be traced to not having the corners 'positioned' correctly. Excess stretch in the corners will have the effect of thinning the texture of the lips and will result in a thin 'pinched' tone and a lack of flexibility. And this so-called 'smile system' invariably leads to mouthpiece pressure. Vice versa, if the corners are allowed to move in towards the centre, this will tend to push the centre of the lips away from the teeth and into the mouthpiece, resulting in distorted, fuzzy tone, sloppy tonguing, and also a lack of flexibility and poor intonation. Again, any excessive concentration of effort in the corners indicates that there is a corresponding lack of attention (muscular control) in the centre of the lips. Puffed-out cheeks also indicate this and must be avoided.

Extending the register

In the task of building a fluent and smooth technique and capability in all registers (high, middle, low), the main thing is systematic training of the lip muscles and embouchure formation. From the very beginning, the student must develop simultaneously both high and low registers, always in his exercises revolving around the notes in the middle register. If he does not do this, he will very often develop, quite unconsciously, a 'double-embouchure'. Such a student will often be found to have a fair amount of control and flexibility in both high and low registers, but cannot combine the two without having to re-set his embouchure. The 'double-embouchure' quite often develops when the student relaxes the lips too much for the low notes (the red, fleshy inner part of the lip rolls too far out) and then, when progressing to a higher passage, finds that it is impossible to pull the lip back in and the tone shuts off. The player must resist the temptation to relax his lip muscles completely for the low tones. This is especially important when playing tongued notes.

The higher notes of course necessitate a faster lip vibration. To accomplish this the aperture must be decreased in size and at the same time the lip muscles surrounding or bordering on the aperture must be hardened so that there is more 'snap' in them. My own lip-movement formula for effecting this change in the lips is: (1) a slight rolling in of the upper lip (2) pulling the upper lip backwards against the teeth (imagining that I am trying to push my teeth into my mouth with the lips—but not by mouthpiece pressure), and (3) a balanced tension of the muscles of both lips pressing against each other—but still attempting to retain the basic reed-shaped hole. In progressing downwards, there would be a gradual relaxation of these three basic lip movements.

Along with these lip movements there must be a corresponding movement of the tongue. In the matter of tone production, the inside of the mouth and the throat cavity resemble the organ pipe; a large tone chamber for the lower notes and a smaller air cavity for the higher ones. Thus, as one proceeds from the lower register to the higher the tongue should be gradually raised in the mouth as shown in Figs. 6A–C.

A few years back, a friend of mine—a lead trumpeter in one of America's jazz bands—told me that to play high notes one must think 'high', and I have personally found this very valuable.

Several years ago the 'pivot' system gained quite undeserved popularity, which was fortunately short lived. According to that theory, the player would tilt either his instrument or his head or both in an effort to improve flexibility in the different registers. But obviously this manner of playing simply takes the mouthpiece pressure off one lip and directs it to the other. It is thus a valueless device, and players who have used it or must use it are those who do not have correct control of their embouchures and who are desperately attempting to transfer the drudgery of toil on to the instrument in lieu of their weak and undeveloped embouchures.

Fig 6

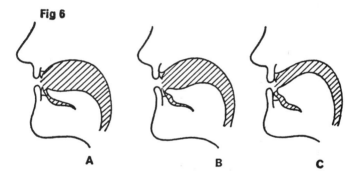

A   B   C

Concerning mouthpiece pressure

The only use of mouthpiece pressure on the lip should be to prevent air from escaping between the lips and the mouthpiece. There is no 'non-pressure' system of playing trumpet, contrary to what some teachers would have one believe. There is, however, a 'light-pressure' system, and this is what the student must attempt to develop. A slight pressure helps to focus all the air into the mouthpiece. This is all that is needed: more is too much. With a light pressure, the lip muscles can be contracted and relaxed freely, which is impossible if there is a great force of pressure clamping the lips down. The pressure must be distributed evenly over both lips.

In the practice period, and as often as possible in actual performance, the player must relax the mouthpiece pressure from the lips, removing the mouthpiece from the lip and letting the blood circulate freely through the lip, thereby rejuvenating it.

The trumpeter will discover that there will be passages, though very rarely, when a reasonable amount of extra pressure applied to the lips will facilitate his playing. This is all the more reason not to use a great deal of pressure normally; for if it is used continually, it cannot be reserved for specially difficult passages.

Excess pressure can result from various causes. Three of the main causes are: (1) use of the 'smile system' which thins the lip texture, making it inflexible and weak, (2) other embouchure difficulties where there is not sufficient control in the centre (i.e. too much tension in the corners, or upper lip not being rolled in enough), and (3) the attempts of young students, whose lip muscles are not sufficiently developed even though they have a correct embouchure formation, to play in the high register before they are physically capable of it. One word of warning: the pressure habit, once started, is most difficult to break!

The lips must maintain a constant condition of mobility. Thus I strongly advise the student to play with a 'wet' embouchure. This allows for more minute and rapid changes in the lips. A student accustomed to playing with a 'dry' embouchure may at first find this a bit difficult, but within a few weeks he will discover a greater ease of performance.

Intonation

Of course many factors enter into the problem of intonation; and generally this subject will be treated in a subsequent chapter. My intention here is to merely point out the relationship of embouchure to intonation.

The embouchure, besides being a contrivance to make a note speak, must be continually engaged in making those notes sound the correct pitch. The trumpeter must have a very intimate knowledge of which notes on his own instrument are out-of-tune and must be favoured, and also to what extent his lips must function to pull those out-of-tune notes into correct pitch. A weak embouchure generally will result in the low register being flat because the lip muscles are not held firm. In an attempt to acquire sufficient lip tension to make the upper notes speak, the player with a badly-formed embouchure often over-estimates the amount of tension needed and pinches his lips together, with the result that the high register is then too sharp. Even though the 4th partial (middle E, E♭, and D) is acknowledged to be slightly flat, I often hear players perform these particular notes horribly out-of-tune simply because their lip position is bad. If the equipment they are using is good, then these notes can be pulled into proper pitch quite easily providing the embouchure is correctly formed. Usually in such a case it is a matter of the player not having his upper lip rolled in sufficiently. If the upper lip is 'blown' out and protrudes into the mouthpiece, then no amount of lip tension will suffice to bring these notes into proper tune.

Bad endurance also can often be traced to the embouchure in its important function of keeping pitch. If the player's lip formation is fairly well developed and he plays with diaphragm support, has good control over all registers, etc., he may be simply playing on the sharp side of all the notes. By constantly pinching each tone, the lip soon becomes tired. This player might try pushing his tuning slides in further, relaxing his embouchure generally throughout the whole compass of the instrument, and intentionally trying to play at the lower edge of the note by using a larger aperture. Players who are unfortunate in having to play with others whose intonation is not good, will soon find their endurance reduced for the same reason. The lips are very busy indeed in simply trying to make the notes speak and to produce a good sound on the trumpet, and if they must also work overtime trying to warp every note into proper pitch, they will soon become fatigued.

I have in the past heard many quite successful trumpeters in good positions, who, if they were given an individual solfeggio test, would probably flunk out! Nevertheless they are successful because they are technically competent and are intimately familiar with their instruments and their embouchures and they are saved by the fact that the sound of discordant 'beats' tells them evidently when they are 'intonationally' right or wrong. This leads me to the conclusion that, though there is certainly no substitute for a good ear (pitch consciousness), the player who has a complete knowledge of his instrument and a sharp awareness of correct lip movement should have at least little trouble with intonation, if he is using a good instrument and mouthpiece.

General exercises for building a good embouchure

Any trumpet student who is seriously engaged in improving his embouchure should have two very valuable pieces of equipment and should use them daily in his embouchure study: (1) a mirror, and (2) an embouchure 'visualizer'[1] or cutaway rim of a trumpet mouthpiece. These two articles will simplify greatly the study of embouchure, since by visual means the student can clear up questions about proper lip function that, at best, without them, remains but a vague conception of what the embouchure looks like and how it is performing.

Lip muscles are no different in any respect from other body muscles and when they have been idle for any length of time, or if they have been overworked, a massage is in order. Thus, it is my contention that a few minutes of 'buzzing' on the mouthpiece prior to all other practice or playing is of inestimable value.

After this pre-warm-up with just the mouthpiece, all students should include in their daily warm-up routine both lip slur exercises and long tone studies. By using the same valve combination over a given slur, and playing the same exercise, with rest, with all seven valve combinations (open, 2, 1, 12, 23, 13, 123) the student will gradually loosen up his embouchure and gain the flexibility needed in his work or daily practice. In playing these lip slurs, he must make the lip do all the work and remember not to resort to

[1] An 'Embouchure Visualizer' is manufactured by the Vincent Bach Corporation—U.S.A. It is simply an average trumpet mouthpiece rim with a short handle attached to it for easier holding.

pressure or force of any kind. He should attempt to make these slurs as smooth and rhythmically correct as possible. All lip slurs should begin in the middle register, so that the student will not fall into the double-embouchure habit. In order to increase his playing range, he should extend these lip slurs up as far as possible until the tone becomes a 'static' tone or squeak and finally tapers off to nothing, again remembering not to resort to pressure. For instance, if a player can squeak a high F with virtually no pressure, he will find that with the usual amount of light pressure and proper breath support he can consistently depend on a high C. And the farther these squeaks or static-tones extend, the greater the normal dependable playing range will become.

Long notes played ($<$ $>$) require accurate lip control if the crescendo and decrescendo are to be balanced and the tone does not change its character or colour. In progressing to a louder dynamic marking or a softer one, the lips should remain as stationary as possible with the air pressure making most of the change in volume. These exercises should begin as softly as possible (but with a good clear attack) and taper off likewise. There must be no change in the intonation of the tone in the crescendo and decrescendo.

All trumpet students must include these exercises in their daily warm-up period. But besides these simple daily embouchure exercises, the beginning student especially must devote a greater portion of his regular study time to an extensive search for a proper lip setting. Only through much experimentation can the student learn all the tricks and lip knowledge needed for a good working embouchure. As his embouchure develops, he can gradually taper off such concentrated study of the embouchure and devote more time to the other technical and musical aspects of playing. Nevertheless, all students must take note that their general progress will depend on how well their embouchures are developed. Certainly, if a technical problem keeps recurring over and over again, it is probable that either the cure lies simply in one's thought processes or approach to the problem, or it is a problem directly connected to some malfunction of the embouchure.

III

TONE

Breathing

Before discussing the tone itself and its various qualities, we must first consider briefly the origin of the tone. By this I mean breathing and its application to trumpet playing.

I think that many teachers confuse their students with their explanation of the breathing process as it applies to wind instrument playing, and some go to strange lengths, with weird physical exercises, etc., designed to develop muscles and capabilities beyond those required for trumpet playing. It must be realized by the student that, after all, breathing is a natural and required process of life. To be sure, it is, in the average person, a quite unconscious function of his body. But the further development of it and its application to trumpet playing, though there is a technique involved, is not unnatural or difficult to learn. In essence, it means simply bringing the breathing process out of the darkness of our unconscious and becoming aware of it and its uses through conscious thought. By intelligent and careful practice then, one can develop this newly-found breathing power to the extent where in performance it almost becomes habitual. I say almost, for it must still remain a conscious effort, if it is to be used effectively and to its ultimate capability.

Let us first look at the possibilities in breathing and the various ways we all, at one time or another, utilize our breath. For our purposes here, there are what I may term three fairly distinct kinds of breathing; (1) Diaphragmatic breathing, (2) Costal breathing, and (3) Clavicular breathing. Diaphragmatic breathing is that which we notice in the newborn infant—a slow rise and fall in the area around his stomach. There is a sympathetic co-ordination between the diaphragm (the thin partition which divides the chest cavity from that of the abdomen) and the intercostal muscles around the ribs. We observe costal breathing very often in a person who is preparing to lift a heavy object.

This type of breathing is a natural means of obtaining more air for purposes of unusual activity. The third type is clavicular, or upper chest breathing, which is noticeable in the physically exhausted adult who has just climbed a long flight of stairs and is gasping for air. I have pointed out the above types or facets of breathing only in order to demonstrate that although the average person normally uses only about half his lung capacity in his regular activity, he does in special circumstances exercise the various parts of his lungs which usually lie dormant. The brass player must learn to use his total lung power effectively; especially he must put into action those parts of the breathing apparatus which the average person rarely uses.

To gain further insight into the proper breathing process, let us look at the physiological aspects of our breathing equipment. The lungs take up practically all the space of our chest cavity and are confined by the ribs and intercostal muscles on the sides and by the diaphragm (made up of muscles) at the bottom. The lungs and chest cavity however are conveniently larger at the base than at the top, and we are aided in our breathing by the fact that the lower two ('floating') ribs are not fastened and are thus free to move. During a deep breath these ribs move out, affording more room for the lungs to expand outwards, and at the same time the 'dome'-shaped diaphragm membrane flattens out so that the lungs may expand downward. Immediately outside the organs mentioned above lie the abdominal muscles. These too are superbly designed, for in the act of expiration of the breath these muscles serve to pull the ribs down slightly, thereby diminishing the air cavity, and at the same time to push up the diaphragm. All of this helps to produce an intense outgoing air stream. This short description is sufficient, I believe, for our purposes here.

Raphael Mendez, in his book *Prelude to Brass Playing*, gives a three-stage formula to remember in taking a healthy breath. It is very simple: 'Down . . . out . . . up!' I shall explain this more fully. By thinking 'down' and taking in our breath slowly and quietly, we should first feel a pressure around our waist-line. Then by continuing further with the same inhalation we should next notice the lower ribs expanding outward in all directions, in the front, sides, and even in the back. All that remains then to complete a full breath is to fill the upper portion of the lungs, at which time the chest will expand outward while the lower abdomen draws inward with a slight complementary action.

I hasten to add a couple of footnotes to this however. Though I have mentioned three stages, I must remind the student that this is a gradual process done in one uninterrupted flow of air, with no hesitating between the different stages. And it is to be remembered that in filling the upper portion of the lungs, one must not raise the shoulders.

Thus we have filled first the lower area of the lungs and then the upper portion. As a result the air is lying on that portion of our anatomy (the diaphragm and the abdominal muscles) which will quite naturally help us to expel the air. We have seen then that this air intake is completely natural, and the only 'abnormal' fact about it is that we have made a conscious effort to use all the facilities at our disposal and are free to control the output of air by learning to manipulate and utilize the diaphragm and abdominal muscles.

'Breath control', as regards wind instrument playing, simply means control of the expiration of the air. Here a detailed and lengthy study must be made by the trumpet student, so that he may learn to use the air as effectively as possible.

During the emission of air, the gradual deflation of the upper chest or lung area will be followed by the gradual return of the abdominal muscles and diaphragm to their original position. This air must be pushed out of the lungs, through the chest, throat and mouth and into the mouthpiece in one uninterrupted flow with no disturbances caused by unnecessary muscle tightness in the same areas or organs. This air stream, with a small but continuous pressure behind it, should gently pass through the vibrating area of the lips (this point of contact should be sensed or felt) and not impetuously blown into the instrument. I personally believe, however, that any further control of the air stream in exhalation is more a matter of embouchure refinement, control of the tongue and larynx (both of which influence the size of the air cavity in the mouth), and purely musical considerations such as phrasing, volume, etc. Thus for all practical purposes we may leave the subject of the breathing process as such.

However, there remain some observations to be made of factors bordering on and adjuncts to the breathing procedure. It is hoped that the advanced student practices good posture while playing, but the beginning student must remember that it is virtually impossible to obtain a good breath and dispose of it correctly unless the body is erect, whether in a sitting or standing position. Air should most often be inhaled through the corners of the mouth. Particularly in taking a fast breath in a sustained passage this must be done so as not to upset or interfere with the placing of the mouthpiece on the lips. I suggest that the breath be taken in as inaudible a manner as possible (a quiet breath is usually more slow and deep). However, when time does not permit the intake of air will quite often became audible, and there can be nothing done about it. Besides, though it may seem terrifyingly loud to us, this particular sound does not carry far and probably will not be heard even by the fellow sitting in the next seat.

The air should never be allowed to remain stationary in the lungs. For instance, there should be no hesitation between breathing in and breathing out. The only possible exception to this might be in 'setting' for an attack on a note in the high register. And with regard to high note playing it should be remembered that a fast expiration will aid the emission of those notes and will to some extent lighten the burden of the lips, thus preventing their tiring.

The type of mouthpiece used has much to do of course with the amount of air required. The resistance factor in trumpet mouthpieces varies a great deal and a 'large' mouthpiece will require much more air than a smaller one. It might be well to note that this is just one more reason why the beginning and intermediate student should play on a medium-sized mouthpiece until he has developed his breath and embouchure control to the point where he can successfully cope with a large mouthpiece.

I have described above the procedure to be followed in taking a deep breath—a full breath. But although every breath should follow the same pattern (down, out, up), that is not to say that every breath taken for the purpose of playing the trumpet must be a full breath, for indeed that would be almost as bad as breathing too shallowly all the time. In fact the length of the breath must be adapted to the length of the phrase to be played; the longer the phrase to be played, the deeper the breath. Inhale only what is needed and no more. In short passages, long and frequent breaths must not be taken, for if some stationary air remains in the lungs for even a short while, a kind of panting will result because of incomplete exhalation. From the very beginning of the expiration of breath, the output of air must be controlled so that one is never short of wind at the end of the phrase, and so that both end and beginning have all the firmness and volume needed. The student will find in his practice that different passages will require different degrees of control—some phrases may have their high point (volume and intensity of tone) near the beginning where others might only come to their climax at the very end of the phrase or breath.

Another secret of good breathing is to breathe in rhythm to the music. For instance, in a slow 4/4 time, if a phrase begins with a quarter note on the fourth beat of a measure, the breath should be taken on the third beat. Good timing in taking the breath initially, and proper breath control while playing, will open up many new possibilities for the industrious student. The modern trumpet player is faced with many long passages written by contemporary composers to be played in one breath. So he must develop his breathing capability to its fullest extent.

The only advice I may suggest in practising breathing and its application to performance is simply to think about it occasionally. On just any technical exercise, test yourself to see how far you can go or how many measures you can play in one breath. Then determine to go a bit farther the next time. Only by taxing your lungs and controlling apparatus can you develop this aspect of trumpet technique.

Vibrato

The use of vibrato and its obvious connexion with the tone must also be considered here. Let me suggest that the student first learn to play without a vibrato. Only later, during advanced training, should this study be initiated. Even in advanced study, the use of vibrato should be limited to those exercises of a solo or legato nature where such a tone is desirable. It is most important to learn to play with a straight, solid tone, without having to resort to a vibrato to cover up any deficiencies in tone quality or intonation. Of course, vibrato or any shaking of the tone or instrument is especially undesirable and unnecessary in any rapid technical passages.

Vibrato is used to enhance and beautify an already good tone, and thus vibrato alone must not be considered as an end in itself. Basically, a vibrato that is too obvious to the listener is already exceeding the limits of good musical taste. And because of the naturally incisive quality of the trumpet tone, one must be careful at all times to keep it under control. Otherwise a 'nanny-goat' sound will be the result. Vibrato should only be used to help keep the tone alive and to give it vitality and character.

Concepts of vibrato vary with individuals, as well as in the different branches of musical performance. Particularly there is a great difference between the type of vibrato used in jazz and studio work and that of the symphonic player. The vibrato generally used in jazz work is wider and faster than that used in the symphony orchestra. Even the typical French classical trumpet player may be readily identified by his particular style of vibrato. Although most musicians in other countries abhor this type of vibrato, one must admit that they have at least developed a distinct style. Generally speaking though, in countries other than France, the use of vibrato in purely classical music is out of place, and at best, it should be used sparingly. In most ensemble playing or tutti passages in the orchestra, it is usually unnecessary and should be reserved for special solo passages only.

An uneven vibrato is useless and not in good musical taste, and vibrato, if used at all, must be of an even pulsation and width. I believe that most players would do well to develop a vibrato of between four and five vibrations per second. There are of course a variety of ways to produce the trumpet vibrato. Some use a lip vibrato, others produce it in the throat, while others shake their heads or their instruments. I discourage students from using a lip or, worse yet in my mind, a throat vibrato, in the belief that the lips, mouth, and throat are already very busily engaged and thus should not be taxed with the added burden of producing a vibrato. It has been my observation that most users of the lip vibrato usually have only one style of vibrato at their command, whereas those using a hand vibrato can easily change the frequency and amplitude of their vibrato. Even in a sweet legato passage or solo, vibrato need not be used constantly. One of my favourite tricks is to add vibrato only after reaching a note and playing it 'straight' for a short moment (see following example). Or, for example, if a

Ex. 4
Trumpet in C
vibrato

Britten: 4 Interludes
(Peter Grimes)

whole note has a diminuendo to *pp*, I sometimes start it with vibrato and taper it off to a straight tone at the end.

I would accept most manners of gently shaking or rocking the instrument for the purpose of vibrato since they may be visually controlled and studied. Preference, I believe, should be given, however, to that method whereby the right hand gently moves to and fro along the side of the trumpet, parallel to it and not sidewards, or pushing against the instrument. Maybe we must mention that in this process, the hand, fingers, wrists and forearm should remain relaxed, not allowing any muscular tension to interfere with their movement. Finally, in order to attain rhythmic perfection and to discover the possibilities of vibrato, I suggest that the student occasionally practice his vibrato with a metronome (mm. 60 or mm. 90) on long tone studies. Certainly the student must cultivate a style, and not leave his vibrato (and therefore tone) development to pure chance.

Intonation

In preceding chapters I have pointed out how both the embouchure and the mouthpiece affect the overall intonation of the instrument. Before going on to a more detailed explanation of the 'trumpet tone', I should like to discuss this a bit more. Intonation has such a great effect on the actual sound of a given note, that the average student (unless he is fortunate in having perfect pitch or really excellent relative pitch), should probably spend as much time training his ear (intonation) and learning to apply it in his performance as he spends on the 'mechanics' of tone production. For instance, in the following excerpt from Brahms's Academic Festival Overture, which is fraught with intonation problems, simple pitch factors assume probably an even greater importance than pure tonal factors.

The trumpeter must know the general relationship of each note in his part to the key or scale in which it is written. And in going from one note to the next, he must be able to hear precisely the correct interval at which he must play the second in relation to the first.

Moreover, to every pitch there is a 'low', 'centre', and 'high'; and generally speaking, the trumpeter must tune his instrument so that he will be able to play most of the notes on his instrument exactly in the centre of the pitch without having to 'lip' any note too much one way or another. Let us quickly note here that the player who finds it necessary to pull out his main tuning slide quite far to meet the proper pitch level, must probably also pull out his separate valve slides a little. I strongly advise against too much juggling of the tuning slides, since after the player has tuned (supposing he has done it correctly) the out-of-tune notes should usually be individually adjusted with the embouchure. However, in the symphony orchestra, and even when playing with fine musicians, the trumpeter may find that playing certain rare solo passages with the different sections might necessitate minute changes in the tuning.

Besides the purely musical problems of intonation, the trumpeter must forever be concerned with intonation problems inherent in the trumpet itself. As we have found in an earlier chapter, to build a trumpet with a perfect scale is impossible. Referring once more to the chart on p. 4, we find that most trumpets are (1) flat on middle D, E♭, and E, and that (2) the low D and C♯ are extremely sharp. In

Ex. 5

Trumpets in C

p dolce

p dolce

p dolce

cresc. poco a poco

cresc. poco a poco

cresc. poco a poco

f

f

f

the case of the former, not much can be done except to 'lip' them up, maybe with the help of the tongue—see the chapter on embouchure. Alternate fingerings, of the D by valves 1 and 3, E♭ by 2 and 3, E by 1 and 2 or 3, invariably sharpen these notes. Though in rare instances these alternate fingerings may be used, normally they should not, for the tone quality is quite different from other notes in this register. The low D and C♯ can be compensated for by throwing out the 3rd valve slide with the finger ring. Most piston valve trumpets are now provided with a 3rd valve finger ring attachment, and no self-respecting trumpeter can do without it. To acquire facility in its use is a whole 'technique' in itself. See the following excerpt:

Ex. 6

Bizet, Carmen (trumpet in A)

Played on B♭ trumpet. Note alternative fingerings
X - - - - - - extend 3rd valve slide halfway
X = = = = = = extend 3rd valve slide completely

Many professional model trumpets now may be pur-
chased with a first valve trigger mechanism also. This
mechanism is particularly useful on a C trumpet, for
instance on the following tones: low E, middle A and E,
and on high A. Many players have the tendency to pinch
too much for the upper notes with the result that the higher
register is somewhat sharp, and sometimes the use of the
trigger may help here. The first valve trigger, however,
should not be used for the low D and C♯, unless in con-
junction with the 3rd valve slide, for the simple reason that
it alone cannot lower the pitch enough. These intonation
problems directly connected to the instrument itself, unfortunate and irritating as they may be, must be constantly
kept in mind.

Temperature affects the intonation, of course, and brass
instruments can rapidly change pitch because of this factor.
Brass band players who are occasionally required to perform outdoors must keep this in mind. And in the symphony
orchestra, where the trumpeters are sometimes required to
rest for several measures or even minutes, often the instrument will cool and the pitch will correspondingly drop. A
few bars before beginning to play, then, the player must
blow air gently into the instrument, depressing all the
valves, to warm it up again to the original tuning pitch.
Distance lowers pitch also, and this must be remembered
when playing off-stage parts such as *Leonora* No. 3, *The
Pines of Rome*, and the many off-stage parts in opera performances.

Besides the study of actual ear training and harmony, I
recommend playing as much ensemble work (duets, trios,
quartets) as possible, for this is the best way to discover your
instrument's tonal peculiarities. Incidentally, the professional player should know his partners' intonation problems and peculiarities as well as his own. This is the only
answer to really good ensemble playing: perfect intonation
and tonal balance.

Tone

In beginning this section, I must first make the confes-
sion that I truly wish I could draw upon a larger and more

descriptive vocabulary, so that I could more forcefully impress upon my readers my concepts of tone. I have concluded that herein lies the difficulty of teaching music students the techniques and concepts of developing a proper tone on their instruments. Much depends upon the student's innate and learned ability to recognize and discern good intonation, good tone quality, balance, etc., so that he can improve these factors in his own performance. And the teacher's capacity to further the student's progress along these lines will depend upon his ability to use words and ideas and expressions to convey to the student an impression of this sound, or that nuance, or the proper timbre that is desired.

The student, particularly the young beginning student, is often so completely occupied with the technical aspects of simply playing the notes that he cannot, or does not, give much consideration in his early training period to proper tone production. I have already mentioned the means by which we may use our embouchure to improve our tone. If we look at this in reverse, we can understand that by simply listening to the student's tone, we may discover whether his embouchure is correct or not. This is in fact the chief way to determine the effectiveness of his lip function and how to improve it. Thus the teacher must insist that the student devote much thought to tonal ideals and production even in the early weeks of his training. And we can only hope that such coercion, over an extended period of time, will eventually produce the desired results.

Another serious impediment in teaching tone production is that of course no two persons have the same or even similar tonal ideals. These tonal concepts vary with every player, listener, conductor, etc. Fortunately, however, the modern student has an opportunity to hear and to compare, either in live performances or through recordings, the performances of outstanding soloists and orchestras and to choose what he likes and reject what he dislikes. This listening process must be encouraged to the fullest extent: careful and intelligent listening to other players in the concert hall and in rehearsals, and, most important, in the individual's private practice room.

With the possible exception of the trombone and some percussion instruments, the trumpeter has at his command a tonal and dynamic range greater than probably any other orchestral instrument. And it is the student's responsibility, if he intends to become adept at his art, to develop every facet of this 'technique' of tone. The trumpeter must learn to play at both extremes of the tonal range; from the strident and boisterous Wagnerian tone to the intimate and subdued tone of the small ensemble. In the symphony orchestra alone, two basically distinct qualities of tone are needed. First, the martial, fanfarish, and dynamic tone for certain brass passages (see Ex. 7 A), and secondly, the more mellow and flowing quality needed in the soft lyrical passages (see Ex. 7 B).

Ex. 7a

Tchaikovsky, 4th Symphony (trumpet in F)

Ex. 7b

Respighi, Pines of Rome, offstage part (trumpet in C)

The trumpeter must learn precision of attack and tone, for the instrument itself is naturally of an incisive timbre and is very capable of obtruding itself even in tutti passages. I don't really believe that professional trumpeters are more mistake-prone than any of the other orchestral instrumentalists, but certainly if at the concert hall we hear a 'goof', we can rapidly identify it if it happens to come from the direction of the trumpet section!

The trumpet tone is produced by a combined action of the breath, tongue, and lips. I have already discussed at length the role the embouchure and the breath plays in tone production. The role of the tongue and the inside mouth cavity is also of tremendous importance. Of course, the tongue is used to start the air flowing through the lips and into the instrument. In this function the tongue serves as a valve, an air valve. Though there are conflicting theories on exactly how the tongue should move in this capacity, we may at least say that the tonguing action is produced by the front or forward part of the tongue and involves some movement of the very tip of it. Whatever the exact movement is, the quicker it is performed the more precise the attack or initial start of the tone will be. I call attention to this in this chapter because I believe that the actual sound of the attack (the moment the sound bursts out of the instrument) has a great deal to do with the sound of the remainder of the tone—at least to the listener. In other words, the 'technique' of attack and that of tone cannot and should not be thought of and studied separately. I mean this to include all notes, long or short. But in a rapid single-tongued passage, for example, where lengths of notes are very short, about the only thing that remains to the actual note being played (or heard) is the attack. If that attack is precise and clear, rhythmically correct, and exactly on pitch, the overall sound might well be pleasing, even if the player's real tone is indeed small.

In an earlier chapter I have mentioned the importance of the position of the tongue in the mouth in connexion with playing scales, lip slurs, etc. This also has a dual effect on the tone quality. The lower the tongue lies in the mouth, and the larger the air passage in the throat and mouth, the broader the tone should be. This leaves much room for the student to speculate and experiment in his practice. One other reminder: think of the tone as originating not in the throat or mouth, but from the depths of the lungs or the diaphragm area. Do not play from the throat!

Let me speak of 'projection' here for a moment. The

vocalist studies it. The string player knows that if he doesn't
keep his bow continually moving lightly on the strings his
tone will not carry far. It is a fact that the trumpet tone
sounds differently to the listener than it does to the player.
I have heard trumpeters play with what might be termed a
'fat' sound when heard up close, but when heard several
yards away the tone lost its 'bigness' and sounded quite dull
and colourless. On the other hand, I have heard other
players with a seemingly small tone who are nevertheless
capable of cutting through a 100-piece orchestra, chorus
and organ and 'what-have-you', even when they themselves are not playing very loudly. What is this quality of
tone which enables it to be heard in all its sparkling clarity
at the back of an auditorium over a whole orchestra? I call
it 'projection'. Certainly 'bigness' doesn't imply dullness;
and 'smallness' does not compulsorily mean brilliance. I
believe that its presence or absence in the tone, like the
bowing technique of the string player, is caused by the
amount of effort which the player finds necessary in order to
produce the tone. In talking about the string player I used
the words 'continually' and 'lightly'. Let us make the analogy
this way. Continual movement of the bow on the string =
constant breath support for the brass player; light bowing =
general ease of playing. If these two factors are present in
the trumpeter's performance, I believe that he will have all
the projection he will ever need to be sufficiently heard.

Contrast, on the other hand, is also necessary in any
musical performance. So there will be times when the
trumpet must not 'project'. Let us note that volume markings are only relative guides to volume. A pp by itself has no
meaning. It only assumes importance when compared to
other volume markings. And often it will assume another
meaning quite apart from that of mere volume of tone, of
loudness of tone. Do not think of pp as meaning simply
'very soft'. Give it some character. It may mean subdued,
veiled, diminutive, restrained, etc.; ff may mean power, or
heaviness, or vehemence, besides meaning 'very loud'. One
must realize too that a Mozart f means something quite
different from a Mahler f. Let me draw attention also to
the fact that as the orchestral trumpeters usually sit at the

back of the orchestra, simple volume markings are of enormous importance. They must 'project' or not 'project' a greater distance to both the conductor and to the audience than, say, the violin players. The following excerpt may

Ex. 8

Bartók, Concerto for Orchestra
(trumpet in C)

demonstrate my point; the *p* (bar 90–101) may mean a 'soft and distant tinkling'—bar 102–4 may mean 'attention —more interesting things to come!'—bar 105: a sudden reversion to the originally vague and mysterious sound . . . but now coming nearer and nearer to bar 109—etc. I could continue, but this in all probability has a meaning only to me. At least I wish to impress on the player that he must think in descriptive terms if his performance is to be vibrant and colourful.

The only function of the trumpet and mouthpiece in tonal production is to amplify the result of the three factors I have discussed; breath, tongue, and lips. It need hardly be mentioned that one may purchase either good or bad 'amplifiers'.

Study of tone

The study of tone on the trumpet should usually be done at between *pp* and *mf*, since the true breath of the tone can be more easily heard than when playing forte or fortissimo.

Besides, a real pianissimo is more difficult to produce with a pleasing tone quality than a fortissimo. In any study of tone on brass instruments, both lip slurs and especially long tone studies must be included. Such exercises, however, must be continued daily over a long period of time if there is to be any real noticeable improvement. It accomplishes very little to decide to practice tone studies today and then forget it in favour of more interesting exercises for another month. Long tones can be practiced at various volume levels and with a ($<\!\!=\!\!\!\!\Longrightarrow$) or ($\Longrightarrow\!\!=\!\!<$). The most important thing to remember is to use as little pressure as possible and still maintain a steady solid sound. Such studies should begin in the middle register and continue from there in both directions. Avoid forcing the high register: go only as high as you can without excessive strain. Only very gradually can one work up to the very difficult high register. When playing these exercises the student must concentrate intensely on exactly what kind or quality of tone he desires and he must take great care to not let any distortion hinder the tone.

One frequently observed cause of tonal distortion is simply the result of trying to play too loudly. If a student whose embouchure is not fully developed attempts to play too loudly, the tone will spread and consequently it will suffer a loss of resonance and intensity. Two other frequent distortions are (1) a shrill piercing quality in the upper register, and (2) a fuzzy and unclear tone in the lower register. In the first case the player must remember to try not to 'pinch' to get the high notes but to do it with correct embouchure, breath, and tongue action. In the latter case the lips must be more open and not touching in the centre if a clear, ringing tone is desired. Any forcing of tones or any sound that is produced by too great an exertion, even in the higher register, must be avoided. The trumpeter must learn to play easily and without excessive exertion and force, for such things will immediately show up in the tone.

Besides long note exercises, such studies as the operatic arias transcribed for trumpet in the J. B. Arban *Trumpet Method* (C. Fischer edition) are good exercises for the development of tone. Or, for that matter, any slow and lyrical song or melody can be put to the same use. Let me here caution the student that any written notation must not be taken too literally. With our system of notation, the composer is severely limited, since many things are impossible to notate correctly. But there is an advantage in this for the performer in that he is left up to his own contrivances and devices to play it in his own style and character, as long as it satisfies the bare outlines the composer dictated. Feeling—the interpreter's way of constructing a musically good representation of the composer's desires—is all-important.

In my own experience as a teacher and player, I have come more and more to realize the valuable use of thought: establishing a concept of tone or style of playing, and then observing its eventual influence on performance. I can only urge the student to develop the capability of 'setting' or thinking the proper mood, tone, and timbre and then transposing that thought or concept into terms of the instrument—discovering ways and manners and techniques of putting the thought into practical musical use.

IV

ON CERTAIN ASPECTS OF TRUMPET TECHNIQUE

When we think about 'technique' as it applies to the instrumentalist, we soon discover that this subject is so broad and all-encompassing that we can only approach it through an examination of some of its components. In other sections of this book, the 'technique' of embouchure and of tone have been discussed. In this chapter I wish to cover some of the other aspects; particularly those which (1) are unique to the study of the trumpet, and (2) are constant pitfalls for almost all instrumentalists.

Lip slurs and trills

Maybe a definition of a lip-slur is in order. It is simply any slurred combination of notes which must be performed on the instrument without having recourse to the use of valves, thus obliging the lips and related organs to negotiate it unaided. As the trumpeter has only three valves (and seven possible valve combinations) to execute an almost three-octave range, such a 'lip-slur' will often be met with in the usual literature. The practice of lip-slurs should most often be done in their consecutive order; open (no valves down), 2, 1, 12, 23, 13, 123. In working on lip-slurs from the middle register downwards, they should be played in the above order. And in working from the middle register upwards (as in high note practice), I usually have the student begin with the lower (123) and easier valve combination, gradually progressing up the scale.

In fact, all lip-slurs must start in the middle register, even if the particular study being done is devoted to either extreme high or low register, in order that the student may learn to use only one embouchure for the whole range of the trumpet. He must not set his embouchure for one particular register, and then have to resort to another completely different setting to play in the opposite register.

There is a great tendency to apply more mouthpiece
pressure to the lip in order to reach the upper notes of a lip-
slur, but this must be avoided. A lip-slur must be done by
the lip! Moreover, the tension and relaxation of the lips in
moving up or down on a lip-slur should be basically an up-
down movement of the lips, not a movement sideways with
stretching at the corners of the mouth.

A flexible tongue can also aid in executing a lip-slur over
a wide interval, i.e. a four- or five-note lip-slur, by enlarging
or decreasing the air chamber inside the mouth. These two
actions of the lip and tongue, however, must be well co-
ordinated. Besides this, the extreme upper and the extreme
lower registers need the use of slightly more breath and air
support. Especially this must be considered in such a lip-
slur as noted in Ex. 9a below, if the tone and volume are to
remain the same throughout. However, a two-note lip-
slur does not require extra air pressure for the upper note
(see Ex. 9b) as the two are so close together, and thus need
not be considered at all in this case.

Ex. 9

I have known both professional teachers and players who
use the term 'lip-slur' and lip-trill' indiscriminately. Nevertheless, a trill is simply a rapid alternation of a given tone
and its upper neighbour. On the trumpet, some trills are
done by use of the valves, and some are not, or need not be.
I wish here to speak of the latter. In the middle and lower
register, where the intervals of the natural overtone series
are large, the lip-slur can only be done by properly executed
lip movements themselves, as described above. However,
in the upper register, where the intervals of the overtone
series become smaller, such a two-note slur (or trill) as that

in Ex. 10 can be more smoothly and rapidly executed by the use of a tongue movement. This movement is approximately the same as it would be in whistling the slur rapidly. For instance, by changing the position of the tongue rapidly (a sort of 'too-ee-oo-ee'), one can, by setting the lips in a

Ex. 10

properly tensed position, play this trill entirely by the use of the tongue. To be sure, in the symphonic repertoire it can only seldom be used. I have used it, however, on the trills at the end of Ravel's *La Valse* and on the end of the 2nd movement of Mahler's 1st Symphony. The brass band soloist may use it more frequently in cadenzas, etc.

Slurs—scales—fingering problems

The 'technique' of slurring or of sostenuto playing is relatively easy to master. Nevertheless, it is in these 'easy' passages that many players go amiss, by not following through with their air support and therefore producing a weak, sloppy sound. The air, and to a certain extent the embouchure, must favour certain notes in certain sustained passages to achieve a really smooth and fluent sound.

Scales must be religiously practiced with the various articulations and styles of tonguing. Emphasis should be placed on keeping each and every note the same weight, tone colour, volume, and length. For instance, in such passages as in Ex. 11 below, the last note of the slur must remain long so that it will have the same character as the first of the two slurred notes.

Ex. 11

The tendency is to play the slurred notes slightly faster, or to 'chop' off the second note so that it in fact becomes a staccato note. Likewise, very often two notes with easy valve changes are played out-of-rhythm with a following difficult valve change or vice versa. In order to gain perfection in playing scales rapidly and cleanly, such studies very often must be taken apart and practiced to acquire a surer knowledge of fingering and embouchure problems. For instance, the C scale can be practised as follows:

Ex. 12

repeat several times

etc.

Scales, moreover, practiced slowly, are wonderful exercises for intonation and embouchure practice. The student must learn the sensation of moving his lips gradually in relation to the scale in order to ensure good intonation and a fluent sound. Frequently one hears a rapid and slurred scale passage that almost sounds like a smear or glissando because co-ordination of the lips and breath and fingers is lacking. One should attempt on such passages to get a 'clicking' and crisp sound from one note to another, not unlike that sound produced by a good clarinettist when he smacks his finger down over an open note hole. This is quite easy on a rotary valve trumpet because of the faster valve action, somewhat more difficult on a piston valve trumpet. Nevertheless it is possible. The fingers (with the tips on the valve caps) must be put down boldly and firmly, but without jarring the instrument.

For the study of scales and of difficult fingerings, as well as that of breathing, I should like to recommend the Herbert L. Clarke *Technical Studies*. This book, I believe, is one of the very best trumpet books available.

Attacks—tonguing

The key word here is preparation, simple preparation. Even players whose embouchures are quite well developed and are in most respects capable players miss attacks and 'crack' notes through simple carelessness. First of all the tongue must always be prepared to make the forthcoming attack. Especially in soft, legato passages which are mostly slurred, and where the tongue has been somewhat inactive over a period of several notes, an attack must be preceded by a conscious thought of preparation. Such an attack requires usually an additional effort concerning air. It must have breath support (the mouth filled with air waiting for the tonguing action to release it), so that when the attack is to be made, the air pressure will be sufficient to start the air column in the instrument vibrating again. In legato passages it is very important to keep the air pressure at the embouchure as constant and unwavering as possible. Another preparation regarding mouthpiece pressure. The slightest excess of mouthpiece pressure 'freezes' the lip in a somewhat stationary position and thus makes it impossible to secure a good precise attack. Thus, if possible, take the mouthpiece away from the lips, even if only for a split second, or at least attempt to reduce the pressure before an attack, so that the lips may function properly.

The actual role the tongue plays in making an attack is a source of contention among trumpet teachers. Some insist that the tip of the tongue strikes the lower inside edge of the upper teeth; others say that it hits higher up on the teeth at the gum line or even on the roof of the mouth directly behind the teeth. Still others favour that method by which the tip of the tongue rests in the lower part of the mouth, lightly touching the lower teeth, the attack actually being done with the centre of the tongue (the 'front' centre) striking against the roof of the mouth. All teachers recommend, however, that (1) the tonguing action must be done with the front or forward part of the tongue, and that (2) the tongue should not move past the perpendicular of the tooth line except in rare instances. In other words do not tongue between the teeth, or let the tongue come in contact with the lips. The only exception may be when starting an attack on a note in the very low register. I will not advocate any one of the above methods at the expense of the other, for I find that I personally will in one instance use a certain method of tonguing and in another a different method. I cannot recommend a certain 'syllable' likewise, for I know that I use all of them ('tah' 'tee' 'tu' 'too') in certain circumstances. I can only persuade the student to experiment with all the different methods and to choose for himself which is the best. Of course more of the tongue will be used in forte attacks than in pianissimo attacks and a sforzando attack will require a more forced and decisive tongue action.

The tongue also must operate correctly in its vertical movements. For an attack in the high register, the tongue must be more tense and arched, whereas for an attack in the low register, the tongue must be more flat and soft. Some teachers advocate a 'tah' 'tu' 'tee' system of attacks in the various registers, low, middle, and high. No matter what syllables are used, they should be more like a whispered syllable and not a hard, forced, or accented one which will produce of course a sforzando or accented attack. Especially in playing a single tongued scalewise passage, this vertical tongue action should be kept in mind; in ascending and descending the scale, the tongue gradually changing its position and texture in the mouth.

One other reminder in playing tongued notes is not to stop the tone with the tongue but by the breath: 'tu' 'tu' etc.—not 'tut' 'tut' 'tut'—the latter requiring two actions of the tongue instead of one. For the same reason, in practising rapid single tonguing do not attempt to play staccato. Unfortunately many trumpet study books (even the excellent Arban) introduce the staccato note too early. Since the staccato attack is infinitely more difficult to produce correctly and with a good sound, I believe that the single tongue study should first be practiced long and with a good firm tone quality. The staccato can wait until this is already well developed. Tone, on any note, long or short, is still the most important consideration.

As the speed increases in rapid single tonguing, the length of the movement of the tongue must be decreased. Even with a shorter stroke of the tongue we must still produce a sharp attack on each note. The trick is to find out how to keep the tongue fairly relaxed in the mouth and still keep up a rapid pace, and good attack. As often as possible, practice with a metronome to ensure correct rhythm.

Triple and double tonguing

I believe most trumpet teachers agree that the triple tongue should be studied before double tonguing. In the triple tongue ('tu' 'tu' 'ku') the K syllable is first thought of as a more or less 'bounced' action of the tongue between two normally strong T syllables. But in the double tongue, the K syllable is found to be an equal partner with the T syllable, which is as it should be. Because of the unnaturalness of the K syllable, the study of the triple tongue must be commenced at a very, very slow tempo, the slower the better. Remember, there are no short cuts to this! An exercise such as that given below will permit the student to concentrate better on the new tongue movement and upon the resultant sound.

Ex. 13

♩ = 60

Tah   Tah   Kah   Tah_____

And from this speed, the tempo should only be increased very gradually over a period of weeks. The problem is of course to develop the K syllable so that it sounds exactly like the T syllable, for the triple tongue as a whole must sound as nearly like single tonguing as possible. Practising just the K syllable by itself is invaluable practice. The speed of triple or double tonguing must overlap the player's maximum single tongue speed. For instance, if the player can single tongue triplets up to mm. 150, then he must develop a good strong and steady triple tongue at about mm. 135 or 140. If the student can single tongue quadruplets up to mm. 120, then he must have a good double tongue starting from about mm. 100. This way, there will be no 'blind' spots in his 'technique'.

Only after the student has developed his triple tongue fairly well should double tonguing be started. It should be

practised in the same manner as triple tonguing: very slowly
at first. The two following exercises are beneficial in
strengthening the K syllable:

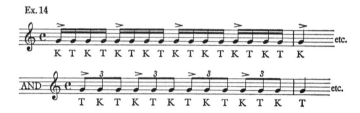

Ex. 14

Later the student must learn to be able to go from single
to double to triple in any order without getting 'tongue-
tied'. For example, the great majority of trumpeters must
play the following excerpt from Sibelius's 2nd Symphony
thus:

Ex. 15

My own tonguing procedure on the following from Stravinsky's *L'Histoire du Soldat* runs like this:

Ex. 16

Legato tongue

The trumpet tone is often described as 'brilliant',
'brassy', 'vibrant', etc., and often it is in one of these

characterizations that the trumpet is used most resplendently by composers. There is, however, another side to this picture. Properly played, the trumpet is capable of setting softer and warmer moods. If many trumpeters have been slow to realize this potentiality of their instrument, composers have nevertheless been quite aware of the possibilities for quite some time. The second movement of the Haydn Trumpet Concerto, to cite just one early example, is written in a beautifully simple and warm legato style, but all too often we hear this and other similar passages played with the same hard attack that we might expect from a trumpeter playing a Tchaikovsky symphony. It is certainly just as important to the trumpeter to learn legato-style playing and to develop a good dependable legato attack as it is for the string player to master the different styles of bowing.

At the outset of our study of the legato tongue, however, we are faced with a paradox. Tonguing definitely implies some sort of stopping of the tone (not, however, with the tongue), in order to start the next one with a new tonguing action; and legato means a continuance or a sustaining of the tones in the melodic line. Obviously, then, an abrupt and accented attack would not be satisfactory in legato playing. Thus we replace the normally used 'tah' or 'tu' with a 'dah' or 'du' attack, which is softer and less accented and which is executed with a softer and more pliable tongue texture. As I have said previously, in legato playing, it is most important to keep the air pressure constant and the air stream moving as much as possible to ensure a smooth style of playing. The tongue must move, but it must not completely 'chop' off this air (or note) stream into separate 'blocks' of air. I can usually demonstrate this more clearly to my students by simply telling them just to let the tongue 'dent' the outgoing air stream with a rapid flick of the tongue.

Intervals—arpeggios

The study of intervals and arpeggios is beneficial to the student in that they are ideal exercises for: (1) developing endurance, (2) improving the intonation, (3) developing a sure slurring capability, and (4) developing the attack and sureness in all registers. As an aid in developing endurance, I recommend the Arban book's interval studies, practised very slowly (mm. 60) and playing each note as a half-note, even though they are written as sixteenth-notes. In that book, the interval studies usually last one line each, at which time the student may rest a few seconds. By keeping a daily record of speed and number of seconds rest at the end of each line, the student can gradually lengthen the exercise and gradually shorten the rest periods. I caution the student to practice this exercise pianissimo. This practice must take place over a period of several months, being very very careful not to overwork or over-fatigue the lips. Using this same sort of exercise for intonation purposes need not be commented upon, except that as always careful listening and adjusting is required to make one note properly tuned to the one preceding it.

The main purpose of interval study for the trumpeter, however, is to develop his attack and slurring capability throughout the whole range of the instrument. An exercise such as the one below can be practised with varying volume markings, with varying accents, and at various note-lengths, i.e. staccato, portato, tenuto. Later this same kind of exercise may be used to strengthen the double and triple tongue.

Ex. 17

Very important also is the use of such an exercise to develop slurring over wide intervals. A slur over a wide interval can be aided by the use of the tongue. For instance, at exactly the instant of making the slur with the lip and changing valve combinations, if 'du' or 'dee' is pronounced very, very softly with the tongue, the slur will sound much cleaner. Such a wide-interval slur must somehow skip over all of the other notes in between which are played with the same valve combinations, and it must not sound like a 'rip', hence the use of the tongue.

Ex. 18

A couple of reminders to facilitate interval playing. The most important, again, is to be sure not to use more mouthpiece pressure for the upper notes. And in passing from a low note to a higher one, or vice versa, the player must take care not to change the mouthpiece position on the lips, directing all of the labour to actual lip tension (or relaxation) itself. In addition, the extreme low register and the high register need an extra amount of air.

Conclusion

A short while ago, reading an article on the technique of writing, I came across the following statement: '. . . writing is essentially thinking, or at least involves thinking as its first requisite' (Stephen Leacock, *How to Write*). I would like to apply that thought to learning trumpet technique. I believe that the actual development of technique is nothing but a gradual process of developing habits, and acquiring proper habits must be a slow and patient process requiring much thought. Many students, coming across a difficult passage, will fight and struggle with it, falsely believing that by simply going over it several times they will eventually correct the difficulty. But if the thought processes are wrong and bad habits are being used, no amount of repetition will cure the illness. A little rest from blowing, and a great deal of patient thought and reason, will cure many difficulties more rapidly than a thousand repetitions. Since the trumpeter must learn to play rapid and difficult passages fluently and effortlessly, any signs of struggle will simply be amplified by the trumpet and a musical performance will not result.

Technique is commonly thought of as speed pure and simple. And we often hear it said of some player who can play a fast scale or who can double- or triple-tongue rapidly: 'My, listen to that "technique".' But if that player, even though he does have a fast tongue and rapid finger reflexes, cannot play a pretty and simple melody musically, he does not have technique. It is a fact that 99 per cent. of our 'budding' young trumpeters will never be called upon to double-tongue the *Flight of the Bumblebee* in public performance. It is much more likely that in the normal course of his employment, the trumpeter will be required to play mostly half notes, some quarter notes, a few eighth notes, and only rarely a few sixteenth notes, with a great number of rests thrown in between them. The symphonic trumpeter receives his weekly remuneration because of his general musical ability, his sureness of attack, and his general reliability and dependability in hitting a few easy notes the same musical way every time.

V
PRACTICE PROBLEMS

In the previous chapters, many of the main aspects of trumpet 'technique' have been discussed. I hasten to point out, however, that this short book does not purport to be a complete textbook. Even if I had expanded it considerably and added exercises, etc., it would still not qualify as a 'do-it-yourself' study method. I know of only one basic programme that will provide the student with a good trumpet education, and that is (1) frequent and regular lessons from a competent teacher, and (2) daily assiduous practice. Without these two things, continued over a period of several years, it is impossible to attain a real professional status.

Most students are quite incapable of adhering to a consistent and coherent learning schedule, and moreover, they are unable objectively to recognize their own weak points and correct them. This necessitates regular help and advice from a good teacher. But the daily practice session must be administered by the student himself. In this chapter, I wish to make a few suggestions which the student may follow in the practice sessions in order to achieve as much as possible in his daily study.

First, the time and place. It is absolutely necessary to find a good, quiet practice room, free of outside disturbances. Avoid practising in an acoustically resonant room, since any echo or resonance will flatter the player's tone (sound) and consequently render faults less perceptible.

All violence and excessive tiring are foreign to good trumpet study methods. It is a fact that in comparison to other body muscles, those of the lip are small and delicate, and thus great care must be taken to keep them in a healthy and strong condition. Because of the necessarily limited amount of practice time each day, the practice session must be executed in a most deliberate and sensible manner. Beginners need only a few minutes a day to start. More time may be added as the lip muscles develop in strength. All practice should be done when the student feels fresh and alert (both physically and mentally) and thus morning practice is by far the best. Always attempt to keep the lip muscles feeling strong and robust.

Always rest proportionate to the effort made seems to be a good maxim to follow. Of course some players will require more rest than others, but that does not necessarily mean that those players are less suited to the instrument. The student must learn his own endurance capability, and practice (and rest) accordingly. When the attack becomes less precise, or when the tone loses its usual resonance, or when flexibility starts to drop off, it is time to rest. Practice up to the point of tiring, but certainly not past that point. Two separate thirty-minute practice sessions are probably better than a one-hour practice session for the average student.

Warm-ups

The first purpose of warm-ups is to help the player to become acquainted again with the feel of the mouthpiece on his lips. Just a few seconds of 'buzzing' on the mouthpiece is the best method of getting reacquainted with it and to 'get the feel' of the proper lip setting again. Warm-ups, however, have other uses: (1) to build up lip strength through long note practice, (2) to build lip flexibility through the practice of various lip slurs, and (3) to acquire a wide range through more of the same. The precise order of the warm-up routine varies with the player. Some like to do long note studies, followed by lip slurs; others, vice versa. Each individual must find the warm-up pattern which best fits his own needs.

All warm-ups must be practised softly and easily, with practically no mouthpiece pressure. Herein lies one of the secrets of good practice. The student who practises softly and with little muscular effort most of the time, will obviously be able to extend his practice period a great deal longer than the one who 'gets a kick' out of playing loudly and boisterously.

Some days the warm-up must naturally take longer, whereas at other times much less is needed. But some form of warm-up must take place daily, even if time doesn't permit a complete practice session. If not, after a short lay-off of even a few days, the student will find that he has lost much of what he had patiently accomplished over the preceding weeks.

Technique—sight-reading—repertoire

Again, what exactly should follow the warm-up period is a matter of personal concern, but any thorough practice period should, I believe, include the three things mentioned above; technique (used here in the broad sense of the word), some sight-reading, and a study of the repertoire. 'Technique' practice can include (1) single-, double-, triple-tonguing exercises, (2) flexibility exercises, (3) attack exercises, (4) scales, (5) register practice (high or low), (6) difficult fingerings, (7) various articulations, etc. I admit that to include a serious study of each of the above in every practice period would be taxing in the extreme. Nevertheless, I suggest that, within practicable limits, the student make a daily and constant assault on all difficult technical problems to keep from becoming 'rusty', or to prevent a 'lop-sided' ability.

Occasional attempts at sight-reading new and unknown exercises must also be done. The professional musician is called upon many times to read through, and even to record, things he has not had time to prepare adequately. The problems of transposition alone that the professional trumpeter must face requires him to be able to think and act fast.

The study of repertoire should be done with distinct goals in mind. This, of course, is especially true in preparing for a recital or solo performance. Even without an immediate performance in mind, the student should daily attempt to expand his repertoire and performing ability; for it is here that he may put to practical musical use the time and effort he has spent on purely technical matters, and where he can realistically measure his musical progress.

Let me digress here a moment to speak about metronomic markings for the sake of the uninitiated. They should not be taken too literally. It is a fact that a great number of the specified metronomic markings in many of the better etude books are all but impossible, even to the most professional and virtuoso players. They stand simply as a goal towards which to work. Whereas the metronome is a valuable aid in the study of purely technical matters, no solo work of any type need be practised or played from start to finish with mathematical exactness, for indeed that would certainly not lead to a musical performance. Such metronomic markings are only noted by the writer or composer to avoid gross errors of tempi.

I have mentioned previously the necessity of taking frequent rests from the actual playing time in order to rest the lip muscles; but these physical rest periods need not be wasteful in themselves, for there are many things the student can do to further both his technique and his general musical ability without actually blowing on the instrument. Does this sound ridiculous? Then let me ask how many 'advanced' students of trumpet are there among you who can whistle or sing through just a three or four line exercise correctly and come out on pitch? There is much to be done in acquiring good pitch and intonation for purposes of trumpet playing, and much of this can and should be done in the 'rest' periods. Many embouchure problems may be studied best by studying the facial muscles and their movements in a mirror, and most fingering problems may be conquered without recourse to blowing on the instrument. Memorization certainly can be done quicker and better without the instrument. All of these things may be done in the frequent rest periods during the practice session without having to tire your embouchure unnecessarily.

Hints on study methods

The student should spend some time simply looking over the exercise he is about to practice, observing key signatures, possible rhythmic or technical problems, and making a mental note of dynamics, nuances, etc. This alone is a valuable time-saver. When playing, give particular attention to the quality of tone, intonation, and to style and phrasing, clarity of attack, etc. In general, avoid a vibrato style of playing, except in practising material of a solo nature. Again, pianissimo practice is best as it is much easier to hear flaws in performance. It is needless and exhausting to play every exercise from start to finish. Work on individual sections and only put them together when they have been separately perfected.

'Nothing succeeds like success.' Attempt to achieve something new every day. The student must gradually learn to discriminate between good and bad playing habits and to analyse his own personal technical and musical problems. There can be no set rule for trumpet playing that will work equally well for all students, but I believe that general relaxation and ease of performance must be learned by all. Each player must discover for himself the most natural way of playing. Learn to play well, but with the least possible amount of effort.

I wish to conclude this chapter by a quotation of Johann Altenburg, whose trumpet method, written in 1796, was one of the first such compiled. He said: 'If one only understands his art theoretically—that is, if he knows everything that pertains to it, but cannot perform on his instrument—he is no better off than the person who only knows how to criticize. On the other hand, if one is proficient on his instrument, but knows nothing about its theoretical basis, he is today numbered among the trade musicians. But whoever has learned his art theoretically as well as practically, of him it can be expected that he will continue to make great progress in it.'

VI

(A) THE TRUMPET IN THE SYMPHONY ORCHESTRA

Paul Hindemith, in his book, *A Composer's World*, expounds the theory that 'all music ought to be performed with the means of production that were in use when the composer gave it to his contemporaries.' He argues quite persuasively that most of the sounds emanating from our modern orchestral instruments are in fact 'counterfeit' to those the composer originally desired. The fact that the average modern-day listener evidently appreciates a heavier sound than that of audiences a couple of hundred years ago has led to an evolution in the manufacture of instruments. This is particularly true of the brass family of instruments, especially the trumpet. Indeed, though most of the orchestral instruments have changed somewhat in this period in appearance and in tone colour, still they were for the most part fairly well standardized by the time the symphony orchestra came into prominence. But the trumpet in use in Bach's time, for instance, was a completely different instrument than that which we use today. In approximately the last two hundred years the trumpet has undergone many basic structural changes, i.e. the addition of valves, and a shortening of the length of the instrument to about half that of the Baroque trumpet. And this two-hundred year period amounts to roughly the span of the normal orchestral repertoire.

I agree with those who advocate the use of the instruments originally specified, and it is true that much could yet be done to manufacture more perfect replicas of these old instruments. Even more could be done by the student who wishes to 'specialize' on these instruments. I am thinking here of the 7–8 ft. Baroque trumpet and the cornetto, two instruments that many of us would like to see reappear on the concert stage. But unfortunately until the time comes that such specialist virtuosi are spawned (and this seems to be a problem of pure economics), the large majority of trumpet players must rely on standard equipment to perform the myriad of tonal timbres desired by the various composers and expected of the modern orchestral trumpeter. The trumpeter then must sincerely concern himself with the kind of equipment he must use to obtain the desired result.

He must acquire proficiency on two, or three, or more differently pitched instruments in order to perform well the basic orchestral repertoire. Very often he will even change instruments in the middle of a composition to facilitate certain passages. I have even known some players who will change mouthpieces to ease their labour where the parts were extremely high or exhausting. But there are definite dangers in switching mouthpieces and this author would advise against this procedure in all but very extreme cases. A few trumpeters can evidently switch mouthpieces with very little immediate difficulty, but the average player will find this to be very difficult and will end up 'cracking' notes or missing them altogether.

The individual player must learn to recognize his personal limitations, the fractional pitch and tonal discrepancies of his instruments and how best he may alleviate the technical problems of his part. An amusing incident happened in one of America's largest orchestras a few years ago when the C trumpet first began gaining in popularity there. The resident conductor of the orchestra became aware of the fact that the 1st trumpeter was using a smaller instrument (C) than the one customarily used (B♭) and he demanded that the player retain the large teutonic sound that was then in vogue in that orchestra. The clever trumpeter concerned simply ordered a special C trumpet made with an unusually large bell. This instrument, seen from the bell-end particularly, had all the outward appearances of being a B♭ trumpet. The outcome was that the player remained on good terms with the conductor, and still satisfied his personal penchant; and today one may order just such an instrument from at least one manufacturer of trumpets. I have heard of another instance where a famous player had a trumpet built in two keys, with a fourth valve added to change the pitch rapidly, which he uses for such precarious spots as the slightly difficult solo passage at the end of the 1st movement of Brahms's 2nd Symphony. A gimmick such as this is not as strange and ridiculous as one might first imagine, for this is exactly the same device that the double horn possesses. Why shouldn't the trumpet player enjoy the same advantages?

We see then that each professional player has his own 'bag of tricks', his particular instrument and manner of overcoming the troublesome spots. Add to this the several different traditions prevailing in the major orchestras of the world and we find that trumpet playing is indeed a fine and complex art. For example, in most German and Austrian orchestras the B♭ is used almost exclusively. There are however a few other European orchestras that prefer the C trumpet, and particularly in France the C trumpet is used almost to the exclusion of the B♭. In Britain the B♭ is the mainstay of the orchestral trumpeter though the C is used for certain works. And in the US there is a trend towards using the C trumpet in the larger orchestras.

To get a better picture of this, I have listed below some works out of the orchestral repertoire with solo passages for the trumpet and have noted my own personal preferences as to which trumpet to use, alongside those of Mr. William Overton, 1st trumpeter of the B.B.C. Orchestra. This list of preferences, then, represent two different viewpoints of the problem of doubling on the different trumpets. And had this been enlarged to include other professional players' opinions, there would surely have been other ideas to to what trumpet is most effectively used on these particular works. These suggestions are of course open to debate, but at least they may serve as a starting-point for the advanced student who wishes to look into the possibilities of the various trumpets. In many cases he will be surprised to learn that he can play a certain passage on one instrument, that on his customary one he deemed virtually impossible.

	Preferences	
	Mine	Mr. Overton's
BACH, J. S.		
Orchestral Suites No. 3 and 4	D	D
B Minor Mass	G	D
Christmas Oratorio	G	D
Brandenburg Concerto No. 2	picc. B♭	picc. B♭
BARTÓK		
Concerto for Orchestra	C	B♭ (and E♭ for solo in finale)
BEETHOVEN		
Leonora No. 2 and 3—off stage calls	B♭	B♭
Symphonies No. 7 and 9	D	D
Other symphonies	C	B♭
BIZET		
Prelude, Act I—Carmen	B♭	B♭
(Written for A Trumpet and includes a low concert E♭. This can be quite nicely done on the B♭ by extending the 3rd valve slide as far as possible and using a couple of false fingerings.)		
Symphony	C	B♭
BRAHMS		
Academic Festival Overture	C	B♭
Symphonies	C	C (D in No. 2)
BRITTEN		
4 Interludes from Peter Grimes (D part)	D	D
DEBUSSY		
La Mer	C	B♭
Iberia	C	B♭
Nocturnes	C	B♭
DVOŘÁK		
Symphonies No. 4 and 5	C	B♭
FRANCK, CÉSAR		
D Minor Symphony	C	B♭
HANDEL		
Messiah	D	D
Samson	D	D
Judas Maccabeus	D	D
Suite from Royal Fireworks	D	D
Suite from Water Music	D	D

	Preferences	
	Mine	Mr. Overton's
HAYDN		
Military Symphony (2nd tpt. solo)	B♭	B♭
Trumpet Concerto	B♭	E♭ or B♭
KODALY		
Háry Janòs	C	B♭
LISZT		
Les Préludes	C	B♭
MENDELSSOHN		
Midsummer Night's Dream (Wedding March)	C	C
Fingal's Cave Overture	C	
MOUSSORGSKY–RAVEL		
Pictures at an Exhibition—(the muted tpt. part in Samuel Goldenberg and Schmuyle)	D	D
PROKOFIEF		
Lt. Kije (off stage part)	D	D
The Love of Three Oranges	C	B♭
RAVEL		
Piano Concerto	C	C
Daphnis and Chloe	C	C
La Valse	C	B♭
RESPIGHI		
Pines of Rome (off stage part)	C	D
Vetrate di Chiesa (solo in 2nd impression)	D	D
RIMSKY-KORSAKOV		
Capriccio Espagnole	B♭	B♭
Suite 'Mlada'	B♭	B♭
Scheherazade	C	B♭
Le Coq d'or	C	B♭ or D
SCHUMANN, WM.		
American Festival Overture	E♭	E♭
SCRIABIN		
Poem of Ecstasy	C	B♭
SHOSTAKOVICH		
Piano Concerto	B♭	B♭
Symphonies	C	B♭
SIBELIUS		
Symphonies	C	B♭
SMETANA		
The Moldau	C	B♭

	Preferences	
	Mine	Mr. Overton's
STRAUSS, R.		
Tone Poems (generally)	C	B♭
STRAVINSKY		
Firebird	D	B♭
Petrouchka—(solo in Danse de la Ballerine)	B♭	B♭
Petrouchka—(duet near end of ballet version)	D	D
TCHAIKOVSKY		
Capriccio Italien (8 bar solo passage)	E♭	B♭
Symphonies	C	B♭
WAGNER		
Parsifal Prelude	C	B♭
Tannhauser March	B♭	B♭
Mastersingers Overture	C	B♭
WEBER		
Oberon Overture	D	D

The cornet also has its place in the symphony orchestra. Many composers call specifically for them in their scores, i.e. Berlioz, Tchaikovsky, etc. At present, though, most orchestral trumpeters perform these parts on the trumpet rather than taking the trouble to acclimatize themselves to a new instrument or maybe just one number on the programme. Nevertheless, I feel that the cornet can in some instances be used very effectively on some orchestral parts and in a great deal of chamber music because of the instrument's inherent flexibility. Such parts as in Stravinsky's *L'Histoire du Soldat* and the short solo in Tchaikovsky's *Capriccio Italien* lie particularly well for the cornet.

The intonation problem of the various trumpets, considering a two-octave range, generally becomes more acute as the instruments get smaller. Much of this is caused by using a mouthpiece which doesn't properly fit the instrument. Most players prefer (and correctly) to use just one mouthpiece if at all possible, and so they do not change mouthpiece size when they change instruments. On all trumpets with the exception of the B♭, alternative fingerings must often be used on the out-of-tune notes (e.g., E♭, E). This will tend to cut down on the player's general technical facility. Thus I suggest that the student planning to enter the orchestral field acquaint himself with the trumpets of various pitches, and their intonation and tonal discrepancies, for their use in the orchestra is at times an absolute necessity.

Many composers seem to be unaware of the technical difficulties of the trumpet and they write in various transpositions quite carelessly. The Baroque and classical composer may be excused, for at that time different circumstances prevailed. Modern composers, however, may not be excused; and it would, I believe, be a great aid to the trumpeter if all of his parts were written, for instance, in concert pitch. Sibelius, for example, notated most of his parts for F trumpet without regard to the actual key of the composition. And he did this after the trumpet had become a chromatic instrument and at a time when the F trumpet was only locally popular. I can see no logical reason for such practice at all. At any rate, the orchestral trumpeter, besides being technically proficient on his instrument, must be something of a wizard at transposition, and the wise student will begin tackling this problem also, as early as possible in his study.

(B) THE CORNET IN THE CONCERT BAND

Having had the opportunity to experience both band and orchestral work, I have found that both fields of endeavour have their distinct musical rewards and their distinct musical and technical problems. If the trumpet is part of the 'dressing' in the orchestral score, the cornet, in the concert band, is the 'main course'. In the orchestra, the trumpeter is asked somehow to blend and balance with instruments quite unlike his own, and at times he merely provides punctuation to a mainly string ensemble. The cornettist in the band, however, where the instruments are more closely related to one another, must usually approach his ensemble playing in a more homogeneous and subdued manner. Thus the approach to the whole problem of tonal balance and ensemble playing is basically different: the trumpeter must attempt to take advantage of his distinctive uniqueness, whereas the cornettist in the band must usually take refuge in his 'ensemble tone'.

A two-hour band concert can be exhausting in the extreme, and of course a 'heavy' symphonic programme can be similarly tiring. Nevertheless it is different. We might make these comparisons of the 'tiring' process to those of the long-distance runner and the 100-yard dash man. The trumpeter in the orchestra tires because of occasional short bursts of exertion. The band cornettist becomes exhausted by a slower (and sometimes seemingly endless) plodding along. In both cases the player must take his special circumstances into consideration so that he may rely on his endurance to see him through to the last note of the programme.

Teaching traditions, study methods, playing experience, and the similarity of the instruments somehow has led most players of both the cornet and the trumpet to accept more or less the same concepts of tone and style of playing. This is unfortunate. In a 50-piece concert band where maybe there are, or should be, 5 cornets and 2 trumpets, the composers and players should both somehow take advantage of the two instruments, and write and play accordingly. A really good band concert can surely be just as musically rewarding as a fine orchestral programme—providing that the band doesn't attempt to play the same repertoire and style and relies more on its uniqueness as a 'wind ensemble'.

A REPERTOIRE LIST

NOTE

It is an unfortunate fact that, compared to the other instruments of the orchestra, there is really not much solo (and chamber music with parts for trumpet) literature for the trumpet that is of much worth. And it seems that just about every time a trumpeter is invited to perform a solo with the orchestra, he is requested to do the Haydn Concerto. There are some valid reasons for this state of affairs. As I pointed out in the first chapter, in Baroque and pre-Baroque music there was no chromatic trumpet. The most popular cup-mouthpiece wind instruments of those periods were the old 'cornett' and the long Baroque trumpet. Much of the music written for these old instruments does not transcribe well for our modern trumpet. Our trumpet and cornet arrived on the musical scene quite late in comparison to the orchestral instruments; and even after the invention of the valve, it was several decades before manufacturers could provide us with an instrument with fair intonation and a uniform tone quality throughout its whole range which was technically capable of solo work. Of course, the characteristic trumpet tone limits to some extent its use in chamber music, as it can be, especially in not-too-capable hands, quite overbearing when playing with, for instance, a string or woodwind ensemble. In spite of these facts, however, it is well known that such composers as Bach and Handel and Purcell and many Italian and English Baroque composers wrote superbly for an instrument certainly not as 'playable' as that which we have today. And with regards to chamber music, contemporary composers such as Stravinsky and Hindemith could write very well for the modern trumpet in combination with other instruments.

Another element which enters into this is the fact that many early solo performers on the newly-arrived brass instruments were too eager to boast their virtuoso talents at the expense of their music. Even today there are several very capable trumpeters and cornettists who are still playing the old 'war-horse' theme-and-variation type solos popular a half-century ago. This trend has obviously influenced the 'serious' composer, and it has permeated into the concert band repertoire to the point where one finds little solo literature of merit. Thus, though there are hundreds of such solos available, and though I believe them to be invaluable to the student as training pieces, I have not included them in the following repertory list.

The chapters of this book on 'technique' were designed with the hopes that students of all abilities might find some useful hints and aids to their study. However, the works listed in the repertoire list are mainly in the 'medium-difficult' to the 'very-difficult' category and most of them can only be attempted by advanced students of the trumpet. They are mostly concert and recital pieces; not training studies. This list of course does not pretend to be a complete bibliography of trumpet solo works. It represents mainly the author's personally favoured trumpet works. I have not included many transcriptions except in certain cases where the trumpet works extremely well and where the character of the piece obviously suggests that of the trumpet. Unlisted also are the many excellent oratorios and cantatas of both Bach and Handel in which the trumpet is used as a solo instrument. There is evidently a whole wealth of recently uncovered works in the archives of the San Petronio Church in Bologna, Italy, which remain unpublished. I have included a few works from the standard orchestral repertoire in which the trumpet is used in an important solo capacity.

Many of those works listed under 'Trumpet and Orchestra' are available in piano score editions. When publishers are not noted, the work probably exists only in manuscript or on microfilm in certain libraries.

Finally, I wish to recommend to all brass students desirous of keeping up to date on the repertoire of their instruments, two very valuable publications: (1) The catalogues of the Robert King Music Co., which include not only their own publications but also listings from other publishers, and (2) The *Brass Quarterly*, a publication 'devoted to articles, research studies, bibliographies, and reviews concerning brass instruments and their music.'

ABBREVIATIONS

picc.	piccolo	org.	organ
fl.	flute	cel.	celeste
ob.	oboe	hp.	harp
cl.	clarinet	WW	woodwind
bn.	bassoon	cont.	continuo
hn.	french horn	strg.	strings
tpt.	trumpet	sopr.	soprano
cnt.	cornet	chor.	chorus
tmb.	trombone	eng. hn.	English horn

tba.	tuba	vib.	vibraphone
vl.	violin	gtr.	guitar
vla.	viola	al. sax.	alto saxophone
vc.	cello	ten. sax.	tenor saxophone
db.	double bass	quart.	quartet
pf.	piano	quint.	quintet
tym.	tympani	bari.	baritone horn
perc.	percussion	euph.	euphonium
tamb.	tambourine	cymb.	cymbal
sn. dr.	snare drum		

TRUMPET AND PIANO

ALARY: (1900) Morceau de Concours (*Leduc, Paris*)

ANDRE-BLOCH: (1939) Meou-tan-yin (*Baron*)

ANTHEIL, GEORGE: (1953) Sonata (*Weintraub Music Co.*)

AUBAIN, JEAN: (1958) Marche et Scherzo (*Leduc, Paris*)

BALAY: Andante et Scherzo (*Baron*); Piece de Concours (*Leduc*)

BARAT, J. ED.: (1926) Andante et Scherzo (*Leduc*); Fantaisie en Mi♭ (*Baron*)

BEDOUIN, PAUL: (1947) Fantaisie (*Leduc*)

BITSCH, MARCEL: (1952) Capriccio (*Leduc*); (1950) Fantaisietta (*Leduc*); (1950) Four variations on a Theme of Scarlatti (*Leduc*)

DE BOECK, A. (b. 1865): Allegro de Concours (*Schott*)

BONDON, JACQUES: (1958) Concert de Printemps (*Marbot, Hamburg*)

LE BOUCHER, MAURICE: (1933) Scherzo Appasionate (*Editions Costallat*)

BOURNONVILLE: (1929) Pendant la Fête (*Baron*)

BOZZA, EUGENE: (1942) Badinage (*Leduc*); (1943) Caprice (*Leduc*)

BRANDT: Zweites Konzertstück in E♭ Major (*Zimmerman, Leipzig*)

BUSSER, H.: (1911) Andante et Scherzo (*Leduc*); (1923) Fantaisie sur des Thèmes Ecossais (*Baron*); (1914) Variations in Mi Bémol (*Leduc*)

CASTEREDE, JACQUES: (1956) Sonatine pour Trompette ut et piano (*Leduc*)

CHALLAN, HENRI: (1959) Variations (*Leduc*)

CLERGUE: (1936) Sarabande et Rigaudon (*H. Lemoine, Paris*)

CONSTANT, MARIUS: (1960) Trois mouvements (*Leduc*)

CORDS, GUSTAV (b. 1870): Konzert-Fantaisie (*Schmidt, Heilbronn*)

DALLIER: (1905) Fête Joyeuse (*Leduc*)

DEFOSSEZ, R. (b. 1905): Recitative et Allegro (*Gervan, Bruxelles*)

DELMAS, MARC-JEAN B.: (1914) Chorale et Variations, Op. 37 (*Andrieu Freres*)

DONATO, ANTHONY: (1958) Prelude et Allegro (*Leduc*)

DUBOIS, THE.: (1920) Fantaisie (*Baron*)

EMMANUEL: (1937) Sonate (*Leduc*)

ENESCO, GEORGES: (1906) Légende (*Baron*)

FITZGERALD, B.: Modern Suite (*C. Fischer*)

FRANÇAIX, JEAN: (1952) Sonatina (*Max Eschig*)

FRIBOULET, GEORGES: (1958) Introduction et marche (*H. Lemoine, Paris*)

GAUBERT, P.: (1909) Cantabile et Scherzetto (*Leduc*)

GILSON, P. (b. 1865): Morceau de Concert (*Louis Oertel, Hannover*)

GOEDICKE, ALEXANDER F. (b. 1877): Concert Etude, Op. 49 (*McGinnis & Marx*)

GOEYENS, A.: (1945) Morceau de Concours (*Andraud*); (1932) Fantaisie Dramatique (*Andraud*); Solo Dans le Style Ancien (*Andraud*); Introduction and Scherzo (*Walpot, Bruxelles*)

GOEYES, F.: Introduction and Allegro (*C. Fischer*)

HILLEMACHER, P. L.: (1897) 1st Solo (*Leduc*)

HINDEMITH, PAUL: (1939) Sonata für Trompete (*Associated Music Publishers*)

HONEGGER, ARTHUR: (1947) Intrada (*Baron*); Sonata (*McGinnis & Marx*)

HUBEAU: (1944) Sonate (*Andraud*)

HUË, G. A.: (1900) 1st Solo (*Baron*)

IBERT, JACQUES: (1951) Impromptu (*Leduc*)

JEANJEAN, PAUL: (1924) Capriccio (*Editions G. Billaudot, Paris*)

JONGEN, J.: (1913) Concertino, Op. 41 (*Andraud*)

KENNAN, KENT: (1956) Sonata for Trumpet and Piano (*Remick, N.Y.*)

MAYER, WILLIAM: (1959) Concert Piece for Trumpet and Piano (*Boosey & Hawkes*)

MOUQUET, J.: (1908) Légende Heroïque, Op. 27 (*Leduc*)

PEETERS, FLOR: (1945) Sonate, Op. 51 (*C. F. Peters*)

PETIT, ALEXANDRE: Etude de Concours (*Alfred Music*)

PILSS, KARL: (1935) Sonate für Trompete und Klavier (*Universal Edition*)

POOT, MARCEL: (1929) Etude de Concert (*Max Eschig*)

PORRINO, ENNIO (b. 1910): Prelude, Aria, Scherzoi in F (*Zerboni, Milan*)

ROPARTZ, GUY: (1903) Andante and Allegro (*Baron*)

ROUGNON: 5th Solo de Concert (*Ch. Gras, France*)

RUEFF, JEANINE: (1957) Sonatine (*Leduc*); (1949), Fantaisie Concertante (*Leduc*)

SAINT-SAËNS, CHARLES C.: (1935) Fantaisie en mi bémol (*Leduc*)

SAVARD, M.: (1909) Morceau de Concours (*Leduc*)

SCHMITT, FLORENT (b. 1870): Andantino, Op. 20 (*Leduc*)

SHAPERO, HAROLD: (1956) Sonata for C Trumpet and Piano (*Southern Music Pub. Co.*)

STEVENS, HALSEY (b. 1908): Sonata for Trumpet and Piano (*C. F. Peters*)

SUTERMEISTER, H.: Gavotta de Concert (*Scherzando*, Bruxelles)

THOMÉ, F.: (1902) Fantaisie (*Leduc*)

TOURNEMIRE, C. (b. 1870): Fantaisie (*Baron*)

VASSILENKO, SERGEI N.: (1945) Concerto for Trumpet, Op. 113 (*Leeds*)

VIDAL, PAUL: (1919) Concertino (*Andraud*).

TRUMPET ENSEMBLE
(unaccompanied unless marked)

ALTENBURG, JOHANN (1736–1801): Concerto for Clarini & Tympani for 7 tpt., tym. (*Robt. King Music Co.*)

BACH, C. P. E. (1714–88): March (Fanfare) for 3 tpt., tym. (*E. B. Marks Music Co.*)

BACH, JOHANN S. (1685–1750): My Spirit be Joyful—from Easter Cantata for 2 tpt., org. (*Mercury Music Corp.*)

BOSSA, EUGENE (b. 1905): Dialogue for 2 Trumpets (*Leduc*)

COWELL, HENRY (b. 1897): 4 trumpets for Alan (*MS.*)

DAQUIN, LOUIS C. (1694–1772): Noël Suisse for 3 tpt., org. (*Robt. King Music Co.*)

FRESCOBALDI, GIROLAMO (1583–1643): Canzona a due for 2 tpt., org., cont. (*Edition Schott*)

HOVHANESS, A. (b. 1911): Khaldis for 4 tpt., perc., pf. (*Robt. King Music Co.*)

LASSUS, ORLANDUS (1532–94): Providebam Dominum for 3 tpt., org. (*Robt. King Music Co.*)

LEVY, ERNST: (1947) Fanfares for 3 Trumpets (*A. Broude, N.Y.*)

MUCZYNSKI, R.: (1961) Trumpet Trio, Op. 11 (*G. Schirmer*)

OSBORNE, WILLSON: (1958) Four Fanfares based on eighteenth-century French hunting calls for 3 tpt., tym. (*Robt. King Music Co.*)

PHILLIPS, BURRILL: (1937) Trio for Trumpets (*Robt. King Music Co.*)

PINKHAM, DANIEL (b. 1923): Te Deum for 3 tpt., org., chor. (*Robt. King Music Co.*)

PURCELL, HENRY (b. 1659): Ceremonial Music for 2 tpt., org. (*Mercury Music Corp.*)

SCHEIDT, SAMUEL (1587–1654): Canzon for 4 Trumpets (*Robt. King Music Co.*)

STEIN, LEON: Trio for 3 B♭ Trumpets (*Theo. Presser*)

TELEMANN, GEORGE PHILIPP (1681–1767): Heroic Music for 2 tpt., org. (*International Music Co.*)

TRUMPET IN CHAMBER MUSIC

(for 2 players)

BORDEN, DAVID: (1962) Fifteen dialogues for tpt., trb. (*Ensemble Publications, Roch., N.Y.*)

DIJK, J. VAN: Serenade for tpt., hn. (*Donemus*)

HENRY, OTTO: (1960) Three Serial Duets for tpt., trb. (*The Composer*)

(for 3 players)

ARDEVOL, JOSE: (1945) Tercera Sonata a Tres for 2 tpt., tmb. (*Instituto Interamericano de Musicologia*)

BIALOSKY: (1954) Two Movements for Brass Trio for tpt., hn., tmb. (*Robt. King Music Co.*)

BLACHER, BORIS: (1958) Divertimento, Op. 131 for tpt., tmb., pf. (*Bote & Bock, Berlin*)

CASTEREDE, J.: (1959) Concertino for tpt., tmb., pf. (*Leduc*)

FLOTHUIS, M. (b. 1914): Sonatina, Op. 26 for tpt., hn., tmb. (*Donemus*)

GLASSER, STANLEY: (1958) Trio for 2 Trumpets & Trombone (*Musica Rara, London*)

HOUDY, P.: (1956) Divertissement for tpt., hn., pf. (*Leduc*)

KNIGHT, MORRIS: (1962) Cassation for tpt., hn., tmb. (*Tritone Press*)

LECLERCQ, EDGARD: (1959) Suite Classique for tpt., hn., tmb. (*Brogneaux, Bruxelles*)

LOUEL, JEAN: (1956) Trio for tpt., hn., tmb. (*H. Elkan*)

MAREK, ROBT.: (1959) Trio for Brass Instruments for tpt., hn., tmb. (*Robt. King Music Co.*)

MEULEMANS, ARTHUR (b. 1884): Trio for tpt., hn., tmb. (*Cebedem, Bruxelles*)

POULENC, FRANCIS: (1922) Sonata for tpt., hn., tmb. (*Chester, Ltd., London*)

QUINET, MARCEL: (1961) Sonate à trois for tpt., hn., tmb. (*Cebedem Bruxelles*)

SANDERS, ROBT.: (1961) Trio for tpt., hn., tmb. (*Robt. King Music Co.*)

SCHARRES, CHARLES: (1958) Divertimento for tpt., hn., tmb. (*Brogneaux, Bruxelles*)

SCHISKE, KARL: (1952) Musik für Klarinette, Trompete und Bratsche, Op. 27 for tpt., cl., vla. (*Universal Edition*)

(for 4 players)

ADDISON, J. (b. 1920): Divertimento, Op. 9 for 2 tpt., hn., bar. (*Mills*)

ANDRIESSEN, HENDRIK (b. 1892): Aubade for 2 tpt., hn., trb. (*Donemus*)

ANDRIESSEN, JURRIAAN: (1958) Introduzione e allegro for 2 tpt., hn., trb. (*Donemus*)

BERGSMA, WM.: (1946) Suite for Brass Quartet for 2 tpt, tmb., bar. (*C. Fischer*)

BOEDIJN, G. (b. 1893): Quartet for 2 tpt., hn., tmb. (*Donemus*)

BROOKS, ALFREDO: (1919) Cuarteto no. 3, Op. 31 for tpt., vl., vc., pf. (*Breitkopf & Hartel*)

CASELLA, ALFREDO: (1933) Sinfonia, Op. 54 for tpt., cl., vc., pf. (*Carisch, Milan*)

CHAVEZ, CARLOS: (1933) Soli for tpt., ob., cl., bn. (*Boosey & Hawkes*)

CRESTON, PAUL: (1940) A Tale about the Land, Op. 23 for voice, tpt., dr., pf. (*MS.?*)

DELANNOY, MARCEL: (1934) Rapsodie for tpt, al. sax., vc., pf. (*Heugel, Paris*)

FRANKENPOHL, ARTHUR: (1950) Quartet for 2 tpt., tmb., bar. (*Robt. King Music Co.*)

GABAYE, P.: Recreation for tpt., hn., tmb., pf. (*Leduc*)

GABRIELI, ANDREA (1520–86): Ricercar del sesto tuono for 2 tpt. 2 tmb. (*Musica Rara*)

GABRIELI, GIOVANNI (1554–1612): Canzona per Sonare No. 1–4 for 2 tpt., 2 tmb. (*Robt. King Music Co.*)

HAINES, EDMUND: Toccata for 2 tpt., 2 tmb. (*Robt. King Music Co.*)

HEISS, HERMANN: (1934) Trompetenmusik for 2 tpt, 2 tmb. (*Breitkopf & Hartel*)

HINDEMITH, PAUL (b. 1895): Morgenmusik for 2 tpt., 2 tmb. (*Edition Schott*)

JACOB, GORDON (b. 1895): Scherzo for 2 tpt., hn., bar. (*Lengnick-Mills*)

KAY, ULYSSES: (1958) Brass Quartet for 2 tpt., 2 tmb. (*Peer International Corp.*)

KELLER, HOMER: (1954) Quartet for 2 tpt., hn., tmb. (*Robt. King Music Co.*)

KETTING, O. (b. 1935): Sonata for 2 tpt., hn., tmb. (*Donemus*)

KLEIN, JOHN: (1950) Sonata for 2 tpt., 2 tmb. (*Associated, N.Y.*)

LEWALLEN, JAMES: (1952) Quartet for tpt., cnt., tmb., bar. (*MS.*)

OBRECHT, JACOB: (1950) Tsat een meskin for tpt., 3 tmb. (*Robt. King Music Co.*)

ORREGO-SALAS, JUAN (b. 1919): Concertino for Brass Quartet, Op. 54 for tpt., hn., 2 tmb.

PITTALUGA, GUSTAVO: (1934) Ricercare for tpt., vn., cl., bn. (*Leduc*)

PURCELL, HENRY (1659–95): Music for Queen Mary II for 2 tpt., 2 tmb. (*Robt. King Music Co.*)

RAMSOE, W.: (1888) 4 Quartets for 2 tpt., hn., tba. (*Hansen*)

REICHE, GOTTFRIED: Sonatas from Neue Quatricinia for tpt., hn., tmb., tba. (*Robt. King Music Co.*)

REIGGER, WALLINFORD: (1960) Movement for 2 Trumpets, Trb., & Pf., Op. 66 (*Peer International Corp.*)

ROLAND-MANUEL, A.: (1938) Suite dans le gout espanol for tpt., ob., bn., harpsichord (*Durand, Paris*)

SANDERS, ROBT.: (1956) Suite for 2 tpt., 2 tmb. (*Robt. King Music Co.*)

SHEINKMAN, M.: (1957) Divertimento for tpt., cl., tmb., hp. (*C. F. Peters, N.Y.*)

SUTERMEISTER, H.: (1956) Serenade for tpt., 2 cl., bn. (*Schott, Mainz*)

TELEMANN, GEORG P. (1681–1767): Konzert in D dur with 2 Oboes for tpt, 2 ob., cont. (*Sikorski, Hamburg*)

VAN PRAAG, HENRI: (1950) Sonate for 2 tpt., hn., tmb. (*Donemus*)

(for 5 players)

ANONYMOUS: (1624) Sonata from Bankelsangerlieder for 2 tpt., hn., tmb., tba. (*University Brass Series*)

BARON, SAMUEL (arr.): Impressions of a Parade—'When Johnny Comes Marching Home' for 2 tpt., hn., tmb., tba. (*G. Schirmer*)

BOZZA, EUGENE (b. 1905): Sonatine for 2 tpt., hn., tmb., tba (*Leduc*)

CASELLA, ALFREDO: (1927) Serenata for tpt., cl., bn., vl., vc. (*Universal Edition, Vienna*)

CONSTANT, M. (b. 1925): 4 Etudes de Concert for tpt., 2 hn., tmb., perc. (*Leduc*)

DAHL, INGOLF: (1944) Music for Brass Instruments for 2 tpt., hn., 2 tmb., opt.-tba. (*M. Witmark*)

EWALD, VICTOR: (1911) Symphony for Brass Choir for 2 tpt., hn., 2 tmb., opt.-tba. (*Robt. King Music Co.*)

GABRIELI, GIOVANNI (1554–1612): Canzona prima a5 for 2 tpt., hn., tmb., tba. (*Mentor Music*); (1597) Sonata Pian e Forte for 2 tpt, 2 tmb., org. (*Robt. King Music Co.*)

GAULDIN, ROBT.: (1952) Movement for Wind Quintet for tpt., fl., cl., bn., tmb. (*MS.?*); arr. Glasel, J., Sixteenth-Century Carmina for 2 tpt., hn., tmb., tba. (*Mentor Music*)

HARRIS, ARTHUR: (1957) Four Moods for Brass Quintet for 2 tpt., hn., tmb., tba. (*Mentor Music*)

HERTEL, JOHANN W.: Concerto a5 for tpt, 2 ob., 2 bn.

HINDEMITH, PAUL: (1934) Drei Stücke für funf Instrumente for tpt., cl., vl., cb., pf. (*Schott, Mainz*); (1932) Tafelmusik from 'Ploner Musiktag' for tpt, fl., 2 vl., vc. (*Schott, Mainz*)

HOLBORNE, ANTHONY: Three Pieces for 2 tpt., hn., tmb., tba. (*Mentor Music*)

LOCKWOOD, NORMAND (b. 1906): Concerto for Organ and Brass for 2 tpt., 2 tmb., org. (*Associated Music Pub.*)

MONNIKENDAM, MARIUS (b. 1896): Concerto for 2 tpt., 2 tmb., org. (*Donemus*)

MULLER-ZURICH, PAUL: (1956) Ein feste Burg, Choral-Toccata, Op. 54 No. 1 for 2 tpt., 2 tmb., org. (*Kassel und Basel, Barenreiter*); (1956) Wie schon leuchtet der Morgenstern, Op. 54 No. 2 for 2 tpt., 2 tmb., org. (*Kassel und Basel, Barenreiter*)

NAGEL, ROBERT: Suite for Brass and Piano for tpt., hn., tmb., tba., pf. (*Mentor Music*)

PEZEL, JOHANN: (1685) Funff-stimmigte blasende Music for 2 tpt., hn., tmb., tba. (*Robt. King Music Co.*); (1670) Hora decima for 2 tpt., hn., tmb., tba. (*Robt. King Music Co.*)

REYNOLDS, VERNE: Suite for Brass Quintet for 2 tpt., hn., tmb., tba. (*MS.*)

SANDERS, ROBT.: (1948) Quintet in B♭ for Brass Instruments for 2 tpt., hn., 2 tmb. (*C. Fischer, N.Y.*)

SCHULLER, GUNTHER (b. 1925): Quintet for 2 tpt., hn., tmb., tba. (*Schott*)

SOWERBY, LEO (b. 1895): Festival Musick for 2 tpt., 2 tmb., org. (*Schirmer*)

STARER, ROBT.: (1952) Five Miniatures for Brass Quintet for 2 tpt., 2 hn., tmb. (*Southern Music Publishers, N.Y.*)

SURINACH, CARLOS (b. 1915): Hollywood Carnival for tpt., fl., cl., db., perc. (*Rongwen, N.Y.*)

SWANSON, H. (b. 1899): Sound Piece for 2 tpt., hn., tmb., tba. (*MS.?*)

THOMSON, VIRGIL (b. 1896): Sonata da Chiesa for tpt., Ebcl., hn., tmb., vl. (*New Music, N.Y.*)

TICE, DAVID: (1956) Four pieces for Brass Quartet & Tympani for 2 tpt., 2 tmb., tym. (*University Music Press, Ann Arbor*)

WHEAR, PAUL: (1960) Invocation & Study for 2 tpt, hn., 2 tmb. (*Robt. King Music Co.*)

WHITE, D. H.: Serenade in Brass for 2 tpt., hn., tmb., tba. (*MS.*)

ZINDARS, EARL: (1958) Quintet for Brass Instruments for 2 tpt., hn., tmb., tba. (*Robt. King Music Co.*)

(for 6 players)

ARDEVOL, JOSE (b. 1911): Musica de Camera para 6 for tpt., fl., cl., bn., vn., vc. (*Pan-American Union*)

AURIC, GEORGE: (1925) Five Bagatelles on Marlborough for tpt., cl., bn., vn., vc., pf. (*Heugel, Paris*)

BOHME, OSKAR: (1911) Sextet, Op. 30 for 2 tpt., hn., 2 tmb., tba. (*M. Witmark*)

CONSTANT, MARIUS: (1957) Quatre Etudes de Concert for tpt, 2 hn., tmb., pf., perc. (*Leduc*)

COWELL, HENRY (b. 1897): A Tall Tale for 2 tpt., hn., 2 tmb., tba. (*Mercury Music*)

IVES, CHARLES: (1958) Allegretto Sombreoso for tpt, fl., 3 vn., pf. (*Peer International Corp.*)

MARTINU, BOHUSLAV (1890–1959): La Revue de cuisine—ballet fantastique for tpt., cl., bn., vl., vc., pf (*Leduc, Paris*)

MONTEUX, PIERRE (1875–1964): Deux piècettes for tpt., fl., ob., cl., bn., perc. (*Mathot, Paris*)

OTTEN, LUDWIG: (1956) Cassation for 3 tpt., 3 tmb. (*Donemus*)

PAZ, JUAN CARLOS: (1932) Concierto for tpt., fl., ob., clar., bn., pf. (*MS.*); (1934) Concierto No. 2 for tpt., ob., 2 hn., bn., pf. (*MS.?*)

RUGGLES, CARL: (1939) Angels for 4 tpt., 2 tmb. (*Curwen & Sons*)

SCHOENBERG, ARNOLD: (1924) Fünf geistliche Lieder, Op. 15 for voice, tpt., fl., cl., hp., vl. (*Universal Edition*)

WEBERN, ANTON: (1924) Fünf geistliche Lieder for sopr., tpt., fl., cl., hp., vn. (*Universal Edition*)

(for 7 players)

BEREZOWSKY, NICOLAI (1900–53): Brass Suite, Op. 24 for seven instruments for 2 tpt., 2 hn., 2 tmb., tba. (*Mills Music, N.Y.*)

COHN, ARTHUR: (1950) Music for Brass Instruments for 4 tpt., 3 tmb. (*Southern Music Pub. Co.*)

COPPOLA, PIERO: (1933) 5 Poems for tpt., fl., cl., 2 vl., vla., vc. (*Durand, Paris*)

COWELL, HENRY (b. 1897): Rondo for 3 tpt., 2 hn., 2 tmb. (*Editions Peters*)

DUVERNOY, ALPHONSE (1842–1907): Serenade, Op. 24 for tpt., 2 vl., vla., vc., cb., pf. (*Heugel, Paris*)

GOEB, ROGER: (1952) Septet for Brass Instruments for 2 tpt., 2 hn., 2 tmb, tba. (*Composer's facsimile edition*)

FRANCISQUE, ANTOINE: Suite from Le Trésor D'Orphée for 2 tpt., 2 hn., 2 tmb., bar. (*Robt. King Music Co.*)

HINDEMITH, PAUL: (1948) Septett for tpt., fl., ob., bass cl., bn., hn. (*Schott, Mainz*)

HUMMEL, JOHANN: (1830) Military Septet, Op. 114 for tpt., fl., cl., bn., vc., cb., pf. (*Haslinger, Vienna*)

IBERT, JACQUES: (1925) Le Jardinier de Samos, suite for tpt., fl., cl., bl., vc., dr., tamb. (*Heugel, Paris*)

D'INDY, VINCENT: (1887) Suite dans le Style Ancien for tpt., 2 fl., strg. quart. (*International Music Corp.*)

LASSUS, ORLANDUS (1532–1594): Providebam Dominum for 4 tpt., hn., 2 tmb. (*Robt. King Music Co.*)

LOCKE, MATTHEW (1632–77): Music for King Charles II for 3 tpt., 3 tmb., tba. (*Robt. King Music Co.*)

MARTINU, BOHUSLAV: (1950) Rondi for tpt., ob., cl., bn., 2 vl., pf. (*Artia, Prague*)

MIROUZE, M.: (1933) Pièce en Septuor for tpt., WW quint., pf. (*Leduc*)

PIERNE, G. (1863–1937): Pastorale variée, Op. 30 for tpt., fl., ob., cl., hn., 2 bn. (*Durand*)

POPOV, GABRIELI: (1929) Septet, Op. 22 for tpt., fl., cl., bn., vl., vc., cb. (*Universal Edition*)

SAINT-SAËNS, CAMILLE: (1881) Septet, Op. 65 for tpt., 2 vl., vla., vc., db., pf. (*Durand, Paris*)

SATIE, ERIK (1866–1925): Toute petite danse pour la piège de Meduse for tpt., cl., tmb., perc., vl., vc., db. (*G. Schirmer*)

STRAVINSKY, IGOR: (1918) L'Histoire du Soldat for cnt., cl., bn., tmb., perc., vl., cb. (*Chester, Ltd.*)

SYLVIUS, C.: (1953) Septet for tpt, fl., ob., cl., bn., hn., tmb. (*Baron, N.Y.*)

WALTON, WM. (b. 1902): Façade (1923) for speaker, tpt., fl., cl., sax., vc., perc. (*Oxford University Press*)

WYNER, Y. (b. 1929): Serenade for tpt., cl., bn., tmb., vl., vc., pf. (*American Composers' Alliance*)

(for 8 players)

ANGERER, P. (b. 1927): Quinta Ton for 2 tpt., WW. quint., tmb. (*Universal Edition*)

BONELLI, A.: (1602) Toccata for 4 tpt., 4 tmb. (*Robt. King Music Co.*)

CODIVILLA, F.: (1919) Octet for cnt., fl., ob., cl., 2 hn., bn., tmb. (*Pizzi*)

EL-DABH, HALIM (b. 1921): Thumaniya for 2 tpt., fl., ob., cl., hn., 2 perc. (*C. F. Peters*)

FELLEGARA, V.: (1953) Octet for 2 tpt., WW. quint., tmb. (*Zerboni*)

GABRIELI, G. (1554–1612): Canzon primi toni—Sacrae Symphoniae for 4 tpt., 4 tmb. (*Robt. King Music Co.*)

GAL, H.: (1924) Divertimento, Op. 22 for tpt., fl., ob., 2 cl., 2 hn., bn. (*Leuckart*)

HARSANYI, TIBOR: (1950) L'Histoire du petit tailleur for tpt., fl., cl., bn., perc., vl., vc., pf. (*Eschig, Paris*)

HENZE, H. W.: (1956) Concerto per il Marigny for tpt, cl., bass cl., hn., tmb., vla., vc., pf. (*Schott*)

JACOB, GORDON: (1955) Interludes—from Music for a Festival for 4 tpt., 3 tmb., tym. (*Boosey & Hawkes*)

LESSARD, JOHN: (1953) Octet for 2 tpts., fl., cl., bn., 2 hn., bass tmb. (*American Composers' Alliance*)

PASCAL, CLAUDE: Octet for tpt., 2 fl., ob., cl., hn., 2 bn. (*Durand, Paris*)

PAZ, J. C.: (1930) Octet, Op. 16 for 2 tpt., fl., ob., 2 hn., 2 bn. (*MS. ?*)

REVUELTAS, SILVESTRE (1899–1940): Toccata for tpt., picc., E♭ cl., bass cl., hn., vl., tym. (*Southern Music Co.*)

PINKHAM, DANIEL: (1958) Christmas Cantata for 4 tpt., 4 tmb, chor. (*Robt. King Music Co.*)

SCHAT, PETER: (1958) Octet for 2 tpt., fl., ob., cl., hn., bn., tmb. (*Donemus*)

SHAPEY, R. (b. 1921): Dimensions for sopr., tpt., fl., ob., ten. sax., hn., pf., db. (*Leeds, N.Y.*); Incantations for sopr., tpt., al. sax., hn., vc., pf., perc. (*Leeds, N.Y.*)

SIMPSON, ROBT.: (1958) Canzona for Brass for 4 tpt., 3 tmb., tba. (*A. Lengnick, London*)

STRAVINSKY, IGOR: (1923) Octet for Wind Instruments for 2 tpt., fl., cl., 2 bn., 2 tmb. (*Boosey & Hawkes*)

VARÈSE, EDGAR (b. 1885): Octandre (1924) for tpt., WW. quint. tmb., db. (*Ricordi*)

WAILLY, P. DE (1854–1933): Octet for tpt., fl., ob., 2 cl., hn., 2 bn. (*Rouart*)

ZILLIG, WINFRIED: (1958) Serenade I for cnt., 2 tpt., 2 hn., 2 tmb., tba. (*Barenreiter*)

(for 9 players)

CATURLA, A. G.: (1931) Primera suite cubana for tpt., fl., ob., cl., bass cl., eng. hn., bn., hn., pf. (*New Music Orchestra Series*)

FUX, JOHANN J. (1660–1741): Serenada a8 for 2 tpt., 2 ob., bn., 2 vl., vla., db. (*Felseckers Erben, Nurnberg*)

GOOSSENS, E.: (1926) Fantasy Nonet, Op. 40 for tpt., fl., ob., 2 cl., 2 hn., 2 bn. (*Curwen*)

IVES, CHARLES: (1941) La Pregunta incontestada for tpt., 4 fl., 2 vl., vla., vc. (*Musical Supp. Boletin Latin-Americana de Musica V 1944*)

LUTYENS, E.: (1939) Chamber Concerto, Op. 8 No. 1 for tpt, ob., cl., hn., bn., tmb., vl., vla., vc. (*Chester*)

RIEGGER, WALLINGFORD: (1951) Nonet for Brass for 3 tpt., 2 hn., 3 tmb., tba. (*Associated Music Pub.*)

ROCHBERG, GEORGE: (1953) Chamber Symphony for 9 Instruments for tpt., fl., cl., bn., hn., tmb., vl., vla., vc. (*T. Presser*)

SALVIUCCI, GIOVANNI: (1927) Serenata for tpt., fl., ob., cl., bn., 2 vl., vla., vc. (*Ricordi, Milan*)

WEBERN, ANTON: (1934) Concerto for nine Instruments, Op. 24 for tpt., fl., ob., cl., hn., tmb., vl., vla., pf. (*Universal Edition*); (1913) Two Songs, Op. 8 for sopr., tpt., cl., hn., hp., cel., strg. trio. (*Universal Edition*)

ZHIVOTOV, A. S.: (1930) Frammenti per nonetto, Op. 2 for tpt., fl., cl., bn., 2 vl., vla., vc., pf. (*Russian State Publishers, Moscow*)

ZILLIG, WINFRIED (b. 1905): Serenade II for cnt., tpt., E♭ cl., A cl., bass cl., tmb., vl., vla., vc. (*Barenreiter*)

(for 10 or more players)

ANDRIESSEN, J. (b. 1925): Rouw past Elektra for 2 tpt., fl., 2 ob., cl., hn., 2 bn., 2 tmb., tym., perc. (*Donemus*)

BABBITT, M. (b. 1916): Music for Twelve Instruments for tpt., WW. quint., hp., cel., strg. trio., db. (*Bomart, N.T.*)

BONNEAU, P.: Fanfare for 3 tpt., 3 hn., 2 tmb., tba., tym. (*Leduc*)

BOZZA, E. (b. 1905): Fanfaree Héroïque for 3 tpt., 4 hn., 3 tmb., tba., tym. (*Leduc*)

CAZDEN, NORMAN: (1937) Concerto for 10 Instruments, Op. 10 for tpt., fl., ob., cl., bn., 2 hn., vla., vc., pf. (*American Composers' Alliance*)

CHOU WEN-CHUNG (b. 1923): Soliloquy of a Bhiksuni for solo tpt., 4 hn., 3 tmb., tba., 3 perc. (*Edition Peters*)

COBINE, ALBERT: (1953) Vermont Suite for 4 tpt., 3 hn., 4 tmb., bar., tba. (*Robt. King Music Co.*)

COOKE, A. (b. 1906): Sinfonietta for tpt., WW. quint., strg. quart., db. (*Mills Music*)

COPLAND, AARON: (1943) Fanfare for the Common Man for 3 tpt., 4 hn., 3 tmb., tba., perc. (*Boosey & Hawkes*)

DEBUSSY, CLAUDE: (1911) Fanfares from Martyrdom of St. Sebastian for 4 tpt., 6 hn., 3 tmb., tba., tym. (*Robt. King Music Co.*)

DELLO JOIO, NORMAN: (1958) To Saint Cecilia for 3 tpt., 3 hn., 3 tmb., tba., chor. (*C. Fischer*)

DUKAS, PAUL: (1912) Fanfare pour précéder La Péri for 3 tpt., 4 hn., 3 tmb., tba. (*Durand*)

GABRIELI, GIOVANNI (1554–1612): Canzona noni toni a 12 for 3 4-part br. choirs (*Edition Peters*)

GIUFFRE, J. (b. 1921): Suspensions for tpt., fl., al. sax., ten. sax., bn., hn., tmb., vib., gtr., pf., perc. (*MJQ Music, N.Y.*)

GOEHR, A. (b. 1932): The Deluge for 2 voices, tpt., fl., hn., hp., strg. trio., db. (*Schott*)

HINDEMITH, PAUL (b. 1895): Concert Music for 3 tpt., 4 hn., 2 tmb., tba., 2 hp., pf. (*Associated Music Pub.*); Kammermusik No. 2, Op. 36 No. 1 for solo pf., WW. quint., tpt., bass cl., tmb., strg. trio, db. (*Schott*)

IBERT, JACQUES: (1939) Capriccio for tpt., strg. quart., fl., ob., cl., bn., hp. (*Leduc*)

JESSON, ROY: (1954) Variations & Scherzo for 4 tpt., 3 hn., 3 tmb., bar., tba., tym., sn. dr. (*Robt. King Music Co.*)

KAUFMANN, L. J.: (1941) Musik for 3 tpt., 4 hn., 3 tmb., tba. (*Hofmeister, Leipzig*)

KETTING, O. (b. 1935): Fanfares for 8 tp.., 4 hn., 3 tmb, tba , tym., perc. (*Donemus*)

LANDRE, G. (b. 1905): Kammersymphonie for tpt., WW. quint., strg. quart., db., hp., perc. (*Donemus*)

LUTYENS, ELIZABETH (b. 1906): Tempi for Ten Instruments for 2 tpt., fl., ob., cl., bn., vl., vla., vc., pf. (*MS.*)

MADERNA, B. (b. 1920): Serenata for tpt., fl., cl., bass cl., hn., hp., pf., vl., vla., db., perc. (*Zerboni*)

MERILAINEN, USKO: (1959) Partita for Brass for 4 tp.., 4 hn., 3 tmb., tba. (*Robt. King Music Co.*)

MIHALOVICI, MARCEL: (1952) Etude en deux parties, Op. 64 for 2 tpt., 2 cl., bn., tmb., tba., cel., pf., perc. (*Heugel*, Paris)

MILHAUD, DARIUS: (1923) Création du Monde for 2 tpt., 2 fl., ob., 2 cl., bn., hn., tmb., al. sax., tym., perc., 2 vl., vc., pf. (*Eschig*); (1921) L'Homme et son Desir for 2 tpt., picc., fl., ob., eng. hn., cl., bass cl., bn., hn., perc., hp., strg. quint. (*Universal Edition*)

NAGEL, ROBT.: Divertimento for ten winds for 2 tpt., fl., ob., cl., bn., 2 hn., tmb., tba. (*American Composers' Alliance*)

OTTERLOO, W. VAN (b. 1907): Intrada for 4 tpt., 4 hn., bn., 4 tmb., tba., tym., perc. (*Donemus*)

PITTALUGA, GUSTAVO: (1935) Petite Suite for tpt., fl., cl., bn., tmb., hp., strg. quart. (*Leduc*)

PLUISTER, S. (b. 1913): Divertimento for tpt., 2 fl., ob., cl., hn., bn., tba., db., perc. (*Donemus*)

POULENC, FRANCIS (b. 1935): Suite Française for 2 tpt., 3 tmb., 2 ob., 2 bn., perc., pf. (*Durand*)

RAUTAVAARA, EINO: (1958) A Requiem of our Time for 4 tpt., 4 hn., 3 tmb., bar., tba., tym., perc. (*Robt. King Music Co*)

READ, GARDNER: (1950) Sound Piece for Brass & Percussion, Op. 82 for 4 tpt., 4 hn., 3 tmb., bar., 2 tba., tym., perc. (*Robt. King Music Co.*)

RIETI, VITTORIO (b. 1898): Madrigal for tpt., WW. quint., strg. quint., pf. (*Salabert*)

SCHULLER, GUNTHER (b. 1925): Symphony for Brass for 6 tpt., 4 hn., 3 tmb., bar., 2 tba., tym. (*Malcolm, N.Y.*)

SCOTT, WAYNE: (1956) Rondo Giojoso for 3 tpt., 4 hn., 4 tmb., bar., tba., tym., perc. (*Robt. King Music Co.*)

STRAVINSKY, IGOR (b. 1882): Ragtime for tpt., fl., cl., hn., tmb., 2 vl., vla., cb., cymbalu, perc. (*Chester, Ltd.*)

THOMSON, VIRGIL: (1959) Fanfare for France for 3 tpt., 4 hn., 3 tmb., perc. (*Boosey & Hawkes, N.Y.*)

TOMASI, H. (b. 1901): Fanfare liturgiques for 3 tpt., 4 hn., 4 tmb, tba, tym. (*Leduc*)

VARÈSE, E. (b. 1885): Hyperprism for 2 tpt., fl., cl., 3 hn., 2 tmb., perc. (*Curwen*); (1925) Integrales for 2 tpt., 2 picc., 2 cl., ob., hn., 3 tmb, 4 perc. (*Ricordi*)

WOOLEN, RUSSELL: (1957) Triptych for Brass Choir, Op. 34 for 4 tpt., 2 hn., 3 tmb., tba. (*Edition Peters*)

TRUMPET AND ORCHESTRA

Including concerti, sonatas and some standard orchestral works with important solos for trumpet, and including chamber works with predominantly string accompaniment.

ADDISON, J.: (1951) Concerto for Trumpet (*J. Williams, London*)

ALBINONI, TOMASO (1671–1750): Concerto for Trumpet and Strings (transcription) (*MS.*)

ALBRECHTSBERGER, J.: (1771) Concertino for Trumpet in E♭ (*MS.*)

ALGRIMM, HANS: (1938) Konzert in F dur für Trompete (*Leinau, Berlin*)

BACH, J. S.: (1721) Brandenburg Concerto No. 2 in F. Major for F tpt., fl., ob., vn., strgs., ceb. (*Kalmus*)

BARSANTI, FRANCESCO: (1742) Concerto Grosso, Op. 3 No. 10 for tpt., 2 ob., strgs., cont. (*Eulenberg*)

BERGHMANS, JOSE: (1957) Concerto grosso for tpt., hn., tmb., strg. orch., perc. (*Leduc*)

BIBER, HENRICO I. F. (1644–1704): Sonata a6 (*Musica Rara, London*)

BLACHER, BORIS: (1956) Concerto for Winds, Harp & String Orch. for tpt., cl., bn., hn., hp., strgs. (*Bote & G. Bock*)

BLOCH, ERNST: (1956) Proclamation for Trumpet and Orchestra (*Broude Bros., N.Y.*)

BOHME, OSKAR: (1904) Concerto in E minor (*Andraud*)

BOND, CAPEL: (1760) Trumpet Concerto (*Boosey & Hawkes*)

BONNEAU: (1950) Fantaisie Concertante (*Leduc*)

BONONCINI, G. B. (1670—1747): Sinfonia No. 18, Op. 3 in D major for 6 solo instruments (*MS.*)

BORDES, CH.: (1915) Divertissement (*Baron*)

BREUER, KARL: (1959) Atonalyse II (*Sikorski, Hamburg*)

CHARLIER: (1943) Solo de Concours (*H. Lemoine, Paris*)

CHAYNES, CHARLES: (1956) Concerto (*Leduc, Paris*)

CLARKE, JEREMIAH (1673–1707): Trumpet Voluntary; Suite in D Major

COPLAND, AARON: (1941) Quiet City for tpt., eng. hn., strgs. (*Boosey & Hawkes*)

CORELLI, ARCANGELO (1653–1713): Sonata for Trumpet, Violins, & Basso Continuo (*MS.*)

DELERUE, G.: (1951) Concertino (*Leduc*)

DESENCLOS: (1953) Incantation, Thrène, et Danse (*Leduc*)

DESPORTES: (1949) Concerto (*Andraud*)

DUBOIS, PIERRE M.: (1959) Concertino (*Leduc*)

GABRIELI, D. (1650-90): Trumpet Sonata (*MS.*)

GIANNINI: (1948) Concerto for Trumpet (*Remick*)

GIBBONS, ORLANDO: (1955) Suite for Trumpet & Strings (*J. Williams, London*)

HANDEL, G. F. (1685–1759): Tromba-Suite (*Hinnenthal, Bielefeld*); (1742) Messiah—'The Trumpet Shall Sound'

HARTLEY, WALTER S.: (1956) Sonatina (*Rochester Music Pub., N.Y.*)

HAYDN, JOSEF: (1796) Concerto for Trumpet (*Boosey & Hawkes*)

HAYDN, MICHAEL (1737–1806): Trompeten Konzert in D-dur

HUMMEL (1778–1837): Trumpet Concerto (*Robt. King Music Co.*)

HINDEMITH, PAUL: (1949) Concerto for Trumpet, Bassoon, and String Orch. (*Schott, Mainz*)

HUMPHRIES, JOHN (d. 1730): Trumpet Concerto, Op. 2 (*MS.*); Concerto XII, Op. 3 for Trumpet & Strings (*MS.*)

IBERT, JACQUES: (1930) Divertissement pour Orchestre de Chambre for tpt., fl., cl., bn., hn., tmb., perc., pf., strgs. (*Durand, Paris*)

IVES, CHARLES: (1908) The Unanswered Question for tpt, 4 fl., strgs. (*Southern Music Pub. Co.*)

JACCHINI, GIUSEPPI: Sonata No. 5 in D Major (*MS.*)

JOLIVET, ANDRE: (1948) Concertino (*Durand*)

KAMINSKI, JOSEPH: (1952) Concertino for Trumpet (*Israeli Music Pub.*)

KOX, HANS: (1956) Concertante Muziek for tpt., hn., tmb., orch. (*Donemus*)

LATHAM, WM. P.: (1951) Suite for Trumpet & Strings (*Theo. Presser*)

MARTIN, FRANK: (1949) Concerto pour 7 instruments à vent, perc. & strgs. (*Universal Edition*)

MAYER, WM.: (1959) Concert Piece (*Boosey & Hawkes*)

MILHAUD, DARIUS: (1959) Symphonie Concertante for tpt., bn., hn., cb., orch. (*Heugel, Paris*)

MOLTER, JOHANN (?–1765): Concerto No. 2 in D Major (*MS.*)

MOZART, LEOPOLD: (1762) Concerto for D Trumpet (*Kistner & Siegel*)

MUDGE, RICHARD: (1760) Trumpet Concerto (*MS.*)

NAGEL, ROBERT: Concerto for Trumpet & Strings, Op. 8 (*MS.?*)

PAKHMUTOVA, ALEXANDRA: Concerto in Eb minor for Trumpet & Orch. (*Moscow State Pub.*)

PANUFNIK, ANDRZEJ: (1956) Concerto in modo antico for tpt., hp., strgs, tym. (*Hawkes & Son, London*)

PERSICHETTI, V.: (1948) The Hollow Men (*Elkan-Vogel*)

PILSS, KARL: (1934) Concerto (*Associated Music Pub.*)

PORRINO: (1936) Concertino (*Andraud*)

PURCELL, HENRY: (1695) Trumpet Overture from the Indian Queen; Sonata for Trumpet & Strings (*Musica Rara, London*); (1695) Duke of Gloucester's Birthday Ode: Overt.

RESPIGHI, O.: (1934) Concerto á cinque for tpt., ob., vl., cb., pf., strgs. (*Ricordi, Milan*)

RIISAGER: (1935) Concertino, Op. 29 (*W. Hansen, Denmark*)

ROGER, KURT G.: (1954) Concerto grosso No. 1 for solo tpt., tym., strgs. (*Chester, London*)

ROSIER, CARL (1640–1725): Sonata für Trompete, Streicher, & Generalbass (*Schwann, Dusseldorf*)

SCARLATTI (1660–1725): Su le sponde del Tebro: cantata (voce sola con violini et tromba) (*Suddeutscher Musikferlag*)

SCHOENBACH, DIETER: Konzert für Trompete und Kammerorchester (*Suddeutscher Musikferlag*)

SCRIABIN: (1908) Poem of Ecstasy

SHOSTAKOVICH: (1933) Concerto for Piano, Trumpet & Strings, Op. 35 (*Broude*)

STANLEY, JOHN (1713–1786): Trumpet Tune (*Oxford University Press*)

STARER, ROBT.: (1962) Invocation (*Mills, N.Y.*)

STEKKE, LEON: (1937) Concerto, Op. 17 (*Brogneaux, Bruxelles*)

STRADELLA, ALESSANDRO (1642–82): Sonata for Trumpet, & 2 String Orches. Cont. (*Robt. King Music Co.*)

TELEMANN, GEORGE P. (1681–1767): Konzert in D dur for Trumpet, Strings, continuo (*Sikorski*)

THILMAN, JOHANNES: (1956) Concertino für Trompete, Op. 66 (Hofmeister)

TOMASI, HENRI: (1948) Concerto (*Leduc*)

TORELLI, GIUSEPPI (b. 1658): Concerto in D Major (*International Music Co.*); Sinfonia con Tromba (*Robt. King Music Co.*)

VEJVANOWSKI, PAVEL J. (1640–93): Sonata a4 for Trumpet & Strings (*Musica Antiqua Bohemia, Vol. 36*)

WAL-BERG: (1948) Concerto (*Leeds*)

WORMSER: (1937) Fantaisie, Theme, and Variations (*Leduc*)

ZBINDEN, JULIEN F.: (1959) Concertino pour Trompète & Orchestra (*Schott, Mainz*)

2–4 TRUMPETS AND ORCHESTRA

Including concertos and some standard orchestral works with important solo parts for trumpet, and including chamber works with predominantly string accompaniment.

ALBERTI, GIUSEPPI MATTEO (1685–1746): Sonata for 2 Trumpets in D Major (*MS.?*)

ANDRIESSEN, J. (b. 1925): Symphonietta concertante for 4 tpt., orch. (*Donemus, Amsterdam*)

BACH, J. S. (1685–1750): Orchestral Suite No. 3 in D for 3 tpt., 2 ob., perc., strgs., cont. (*C. F. Peters*); Orchestral Suite No. 4 in D for 3 tpt., 3 ob., perc., strg., cont. (*C. F. Peters*); Christmas Oratorio (*C. F. Peters*); B Minor Mass (*C. F. Peters*)

BONONCINI, GIOVANNI (1660–1750): Sinfonia No. 10 in D Major for 7 Solo Instruments

CORELLI: Concertino (*MS.?*)

EDER, H.: (1961) Musik für 2 Trompeten und Streichorchester, Op. 23 (*Breitkopf & Hartel*)

FISCHER, J. K. F.: (1696) Le Journal de Printemps—Suite No. 8 for 2 tpt., strgs., cont.

HANDEL, G. F.: (1747) Judas Maccabeus; (1749) Fireworks Music; Concerto in D for 2 Trumpets, Hn., Tym., & Strings

HUMPHRIES, JOHN (d. 1730): Concerto I, Op. 3 for 2 Trumpets, Tym., & Strings (*MS.?*)

KETTING, OTTO: Concertino for 3 tpt., orch. (*Donemus*)

LEGRENZI, GIOVANNI (1626–90): Sonata 'La Buscha' for 2 tpt., strgs., cont.

MANFREDINI, FRANCESCO (1680–1748): Concerto per due Trombe (*Carisch, Milan*)

MARTINI, PADRE: (1743) Sonata for 4 Trumpets & Strings (*Robt. King Music Co.*)

PERTI, GIACOMO (1661–1756): Sonata for 4 Trumpets & Strings (*MS.*)

PURCELL, HENRY: (1690) Yorkshire Feast Song: Symphony for 3 tpt., strgs., tym., cont.; Voluntary in C for 2 Trumpets (*Mercury Music Co.*); The Cebell for 2 tpt, strgs., perc., cont.; (1692) Symphony from the Fairy Queen for 2 tpt, strgs, tym.

STOELZEL, G. H. (1690–1749): Concerto in re majeur for 6 tpt., 4 timbales, 2 clavecins, double strg. orch.

TORELLI, G. (1658–1709): Sinfonia in D dur für zwei oboen, zwei trompeten (*MS.*); Sinfonia in D for 2 Trumpets, Strings, & Continuo (*MS.*); Sinfonia for 4 Trumpets, Oboes, Strings, & Tym. (*MS.*)

VEJVANOWSKY, PAVEL J.: (1684) Sonata Venatorio for 2 Trumpets & Strings (*Musica Antiqua Bohemica, Vol.* 2); (1670) Serenada for 2 Trumpets & Strings (*Musica Antiqua Bohemica, Vol.* 36)

VIVALDI, ANTONIO (1669–1741): Concerto in E♭ for 2 Trumpets (*International Music Co.*); Concerto in C for 2 Trumpets (*International Music Co.*)